LEAN SIX SIGMA
MANAGEMENT SYSTEM
for Leaders

LUIS SOCCONINI
& CARLO REATO

It's Not the Big That Eat the Small...
It's the Fast That Eat the Slow

Jason Jennings & Laurence Haughton

TABLE OF CONTENTS

PREFACE

We have observed many times that companies are being managed the same way they were in the past, while the needs of today have changed and the needs of tomorrow will change even more.

Today, companies that continue on being slow to deliver products and services, with inconsistent quality, complaints, rejections, high prices and costs, and insufficient communication are destined to disappear.

In the Twentieth Century, making changes was an option. Now, it has become a day to day requirement in order to stay in business. In addition, these changes can't be as slow as they were in the past.

Companies must learn and re-learn to adjust to the rapid pace of market needs if they want to survive and surpass their competitors. Actually, it is necessary to consider reinventing your business. Fast means also rethinking innovation, product or service adaptation, digitalization (Industry 4.0/Industrial Internet of Things IIoT), sales force adjustments, logistics, e-commerce, certifications, agile teams, projects, and more.

This book has been honed over the last couple of years by hundreds of leaders and professionals whom we have taught and supported to become best-in-class companies. It will help you understand and implement an extremely strong, sustainable, and successful continuous improvement system: *Lean Six Sigma Management System*.

It is dedicated to all the leaders who understand the need for change and want to implement a continuous improvement system that will enable them to stay ahead in business. It is important to know that generally only 7% to 10% of companies that begin a Lean Six Sigma Journey succeed and obtain a cultural change and long-term results. Over the last two decades, we have studied why companies succeeded, while others failed in the journey of Lean Six Sigma. We will explain in detail "The missing – Link" and guide you how to be successful in the Lean Six Sigma journey.

Our FULL commitment with this book is to make sure that YOU will be 100% successful in the Lean Six Sigma journey.

Our work will be to guide you on how to achieve and implement a *Lean Six Sigma Management System* as a way of life. We will use examples and experience gained from hundreds of implementations in various fields and sizes of companies. Solutions that are presented in this book and the *Lean Six Sigma Management Fieldbook (future LSSM – Fieldbook)* are really simple and very effective. In fact, don't be surprised by how powerful they are, even though simple.

ACKNOWLEDGEMENTS

We are very thankful for the numerous people who shared their inputs and insights over a period of many years. The continuous interest inspired us to write this Lean Six Sigma Management System book, dedicated to leaders who are always in search of tools to improve their business. We are also grateful for the many people who devoted time to review the chapters and provide us with endless encouragement along the way.

Our deepest gratitude goes to our families, in particular to our wives Marcella Socconini and Gabriella Reato for all the support we have received, as well as the children of Luis: Sofia, Andrea and Natalia.

CHAPTER 1

1. INTRODUCTION

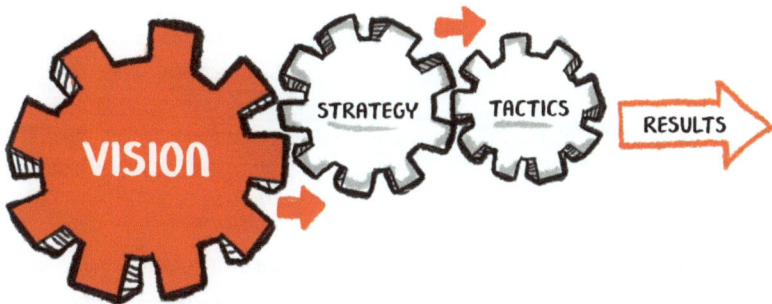

VISION • STRATEGY • TACTICS • RESULTS

1. INTRODUCTION

In this book, we will reference some companies that had an issue, asked for help, and accepted our humble help through the *Lean Six Sigma Management System* and its supporting tools and methodology. You will learn that Lean Six Sigma is not just a couple of tools; it's a complete system and way of life, and not just for manufacturing and largescale corporations such as GE or Motorola. It has been used for every industry and any size, from a one-person street food business up to large scale companies like GE. We will reference some companies in the book in order to explain what helped them achieve certain types of results. We have purposely eliminated company names, not because they don't exist, but in order to prevent influencing the reader by their brand or transformation. We have learned that by not mentioning company names, we remain focused on the company we want to improve.

We will provide examples from the following industries:

Manufacturing
- Medical devices
- Automotive parts
- Food products
- Machine manufactures
- Metal and plastic products

Service
- Hospital groups
- Banking
- Car dealers service and and repair shops
- Restaurants
- Retail
- And many more...

We hope you will find your company in one or another familiar industry. If we have not mentioned your industry, you can be sure that it will work in yours, too. For now, it's important that you know that *Lean Six Sigma Management System* is for all types and sizes of businesses, even for start - ups.

Here are a few statements from company owners or their board members who contacted us and we interviewed, when we met for the first time at their company:

"Well, our inventory turnover and efficiency have increased." However, when we asked them if that meant they are making more money or have an increased cash flow, they answered: *"...actually no. On the contrary, as sales increased, our earnings decreased, and we couldn't improve them."*

"Our sales have lowered and our costs rose, so that we started to think about going out of business." They generally attributed it to fierce competition.

"We brought new products to the market, but sales are flat and earnings are declining."

"We started with some Lean activities, but we have yet not seen the results on the bottom line."

These outcomes are obviously not acceptable or motivating for doing business. On the other hand, we have met company leaders who have worked hard over the last decades and achieved outstanding results with their teams. We were humbled by being asked to support them to become even better. We have had the great fortune to train, support, and coach all type of companies - small, medium, large, and multinational companies, in different departments, such as sales, new product development, purchasing, warehouse, production, quality, maintenance, logistics, HR, service, etc. In doing this, we have had the great opportunity to learn from exceptional people through their knowledge, leadership, and great character.

We have also had the opportunity to teach these topics in lectures at important universities where we have met people from whom we learned more than we taught. In addition, we have learned the way not to operate a business, and that understanding inspired us to work hard to develop a systemic approach.

We believe that a motivation to implement a *Lean Six Sigma Management System* is that companies are no longer worried about selling more, but are concerned about keeping customers satisfied and generating more earnings. Therefore, we can assure you that *Lean Six Sigma Management System* is generating more sustainable earnings than any other initiative.

It is important to realize that before you decide to start a Lean Six Sigma journey, it requires a clear understanding, dedication, discipline, and strict follow-up to be implemented. It will need to be practiced and followed by the whole company to be successful. A fully committed top management is the main ingredient to ensure long term success. The absence of this is the main cause of failure, followed by resistance to change. *Lean Six Sigma Management System* will also require the participation of all departments and key people within the company.

In the past, when a company wanted to increase its top and bottom line, it simply increased its prices, and in this way, its earnings. When the client supported these changes, there was always a way to increase its profits. These decisions were the best way to solve the problem of low earnings or to reduce losses at the time. **See Graph 1.**

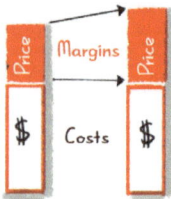 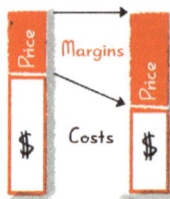 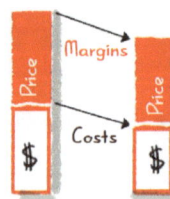 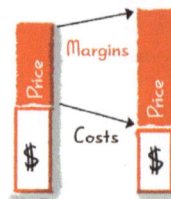

Graph 2: Shows how the same market defined how much it was willing to pay since more options began to exist and the competition increased. Then, the only way to increase profits was to reduce costs. It is here where *Lean Six Sigma Management System* starts to makes sense.

Graph 3: Companies must design systems so that although they reduce prices, they maintain their level of earnings, since now those that dominate this concept are the only ones that manage to succeed in remaining in the marketplace. Then, the cost control and the relation that they have with the prices must be perfectly understood and constantly evaluated.

 **Graph 4:** Successfully implementing *Lean Six Sigma Management System* (as a system). We have seen companies being able to increase the willingness to pay due to consistent quality and service, and at the same time further reduce costs and so increase margins. This version in Graph 4 is the goal of a *Lean Six Sigma Management System* and the reason to implement it in any industry, regardless of the size of the company, whether it is privately owned, publicly owned, a foundation or a private equity company. It just doesn't matter; the system works everywhere.

Although we have spoken about increasing profitability, we would like to mention that one of the major benefits of *Lean Six Sigma Management System* is that people will enjoy a better quality of life, because for many of them, going to work is like going to war; it is like suffering, fighting themselves to deal with the internal bureaucracy, becoming stressed, protecting themselves, demonstrating that they are better than others, and in some cases, even literally dying.

Lean Six Sigma Management System comes accompanied with a better quality of life in those 8 hours (if it really were eight hours), that we are at work; that is to say, a third of our lives! That ought to be a time that is worth the pain to live in the best conditions because it is there where we can realize our professional dreams, which are a fundamental part of our existence.

Enjoy the reading and enjoy the change. Drive your company to be best-in-class with the *Lean Six Sigma Management System.*

1.1 WHY DID WE WRITE THIS BOOK AND WHAT ARE THE KEY TAKEAWAYS FOR READERS?

Why did we write this book?

From the time when Henry Ford implemented his lean concept in his Model-T production line in the early 1900s and Toyota implemented their Toyota Production System in 1970, many other companies have tried to copy and implement the Toyota Production System or similar lean programs.

Millions of articles and thousands of books have been written regarding lean, and later on, about Six Sigma. Both are great methodologies and are best used together in order to sustain increased customer satisfaction, increased level of quality, improved processes, reduced complaints, and at the end of the day, improved results. Leaders and upper management often ask us what book they should buy and read in order to have some guidance and insights for a successful Lean Six Sigma journey.

Today, it is indeed not easy to find the appropriate book or article out of the many books available. If you go to Amazon, you will find +5000 Lean Six Sigma results, and if you google the phrase, you might find more than 60,000,000 results — an amazing amount! In spite of all the books, videos, and articles that have been written, we have not found a simple, complete, and straight to the point book on *Lean Six Sigma Management System for Leaders.* This is the reason we decided to write this book, explaining *Lean Six Sigma Management System* in a simple, practical, and easy to understand way.

Many attempts of implementing have failed because leaders are mainly taking care of contracting some training, developing some projects, using some tools, and expecting something to happen. But, there is a missing link; this is called the *Lean Six Sigma Management System*. That is why many companies start the process, but one or two years later, they come back to the previous mode of operation.

The big difference between this book and all the other books is that we help you implement a real and strong L*ean Six Sigma Management System*, which will be sustainable and provide huge and long-term benefits from learning about it and designing it to fit your own company's needs.

To whom do we dedicate this book?

Leaders-owners, top management, boards of directors, from single-person companies up to mid or large-scale companies, so they can be brought up to speed quickly in concepts, principles, and benefits, in conjunction with the separate *LSSM - Fieldbook*, which will go in detail about real life examples and provide the opportunity to practice lean with plenty of formats and exercises. Leaders need to be aware and understand the benefits of what can be achieved by implementing a Lean and Six Sigma philosophy in their company.

Also, this type of strategic initiative needs to start from the top; otherwise it will fail. It is definitively not enough to send some middle management employees through training and certifications in the hope that *Lean Six Sigma* will bring substantial benefits to the company.

A successful and sustainable implementation of Lean and Six Sigma is only possible if the leaders inspire, guide, and support these initiatives through a strategic decision to include them in the company's Strategy, Mission and Values.

Key takeaways
We commit to deliver the following takeaways by reading this book: and the supporting *LSSM - Fieldbook*:

- Understand the Lean and Six Sigma Philosophy
- How to transform to a Lean Six Sigma Company
- Awareness of myths surrounding Lean Six Sigma
- Step by step process of how to achieve a successful implementation
- Benefits and investments needed
- Understand the key tools
- Resources, dedication, and discipline needed
- Required commitment by the company, leaders, and management for the endeavor
- How to avoid risks and pitfalls
- How to get successfully started or restart step by step
- Benefits or risks with Industry 4.0/Industrial Internet of Things IIoT
- Why it works for any industry and any size of business
- Why you should not wait to start implementing it

Book Organization
We have developed a process in order to guarantee the successful understanding and implementation of each topic of *Lean Six Sigma Management System* in your business. We will typically follow the steps to explain every tool:

√ **Situation**	Describes a situation
√ **About**	What is it about?
√ **Benefits**	What benefits will it provide?
√ **Elements**	What are the key elements?
√ **Roles**	Who will play what role?
√ **Application**	When is it used?
√ **Procedure**	Description of the steps to follow
√ **Time**	Description of the time needed to implement
√ **Examples**	Presentation of real life examples
√ **Implementation**	Exercises assigned to start practicing it

Basically, the first eight steps are found in this book, and steps nine and ten with examples, formats and exercises will be found in the *LSSM - Fieldbook*.

1.2 THE LEAN SIX SIGMA COMPANY MATURITY MODEL

The following model is very helpful to understand how companies are being developed, and how they are designed, evaluated, and improved through **Adaptation and Improvement Cycles** where in every step, strategic, and tactical tools are used in order to create a sustainable *Lean Six Sigma Management System.*

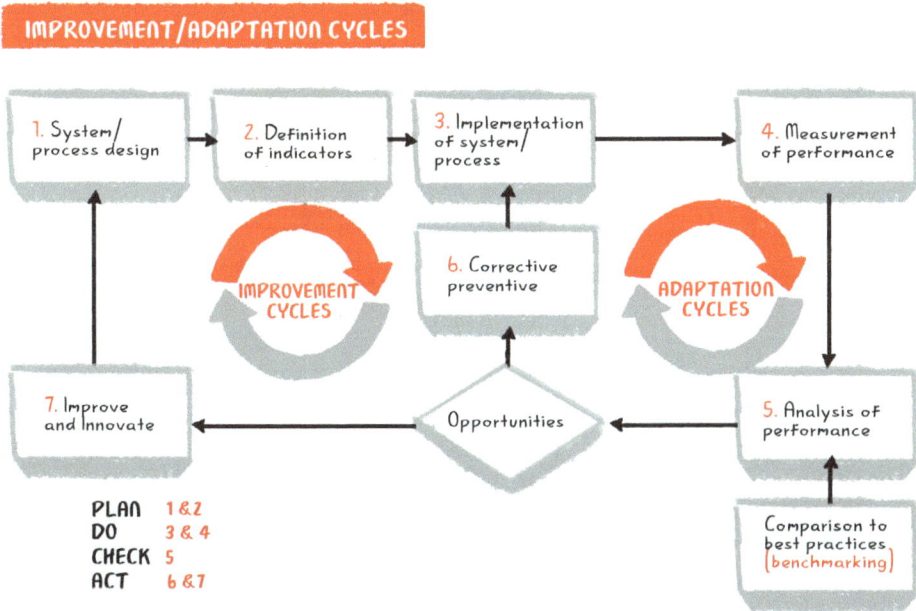

1. The first step is when systems, products, business models, structure, strategies, projects, etc. are designed and created, expecting to be accepted by the market and successful enough to run for the following years.
2. Key performance indicators are defined to periodically understand the results of the company.
3. Implementation of projects and plans take place to develop new systems, products, processes, or to change something to solve a problem or to improve the system.
4. Once the process is running, performance is measured based on the key indicators previously defined.
5. In the analysis step, the team reviews results and selects actions, methods and tools according to the current situation.
6. The first and most common actions are corrective actions due to the many problems or situations that need to be solved in a short time, but also preventive actions are taken to avoid future problems – Adaptation Cycle.
7. Improvement actions are taken when the company is being developed

to the next level in order to achieve higher goals the company has established. These types of actions are also known as Kaizen for continuous improvement and Kaikaku for innovation – Continuous Improvement Cycle.

The numbers indicate the PDCA – steps, 1-2 *Plan step*, 3-4 *Do step*, 5 *Check step*, and 6-7 the *Act step*. Usually, we use the *Adaptation Cycle* for new processes or starting up a business and the improve/innovate for more mature processes.

In the following chart, you can observe the **Adaptation PDCA - Cycle**.

The Adaptation Cycle will need to be repeated on and on, until the performance indicators have been reached. Afterward, we will continue to improve and get better day by day and thus raise the performance bar. Additionally, we can compare ourselves to best-in-class companies in the marketplace and become even better than these companies.

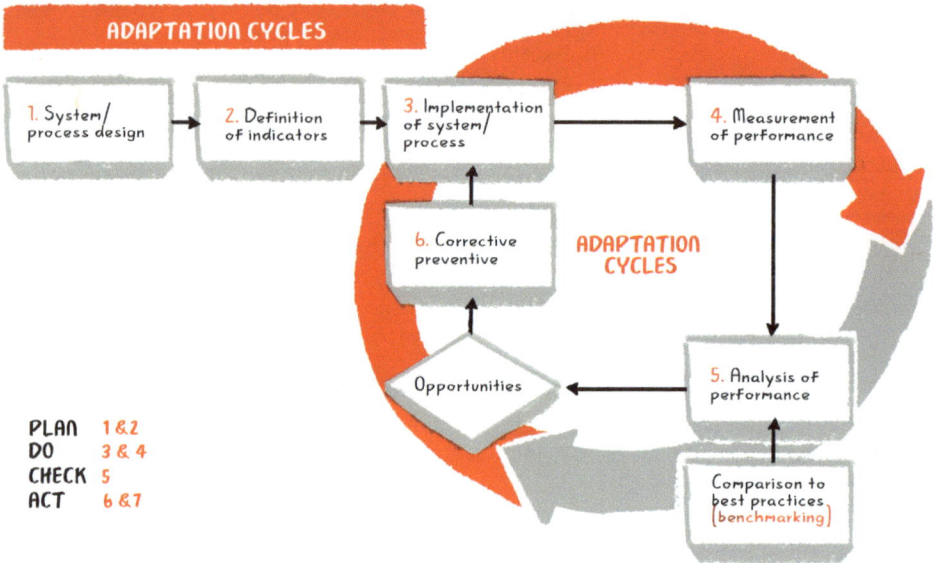

ADAPTATION CYCLES

1. System/ process design
2. Definition of indicators
3. Implementation of system/ process
4. Measurement of performance
6. Corrective preventive
ADAPTATION CYCLES
Opportunities
5. Analysis of performance
Comparison to best practices (benchmarking)

PLAN   1 & 2
DO   3 & 4
CHECK   5
ACT   6 & 7

When we want to make a big step forward, such as a new technology, new processes, or new products, we will need to use the **Improvement PDCA - Cycle**.

This will be achieved through a complete change in the process. After this cycle, we will go back to the Adaptation Cycle to continue to improve.

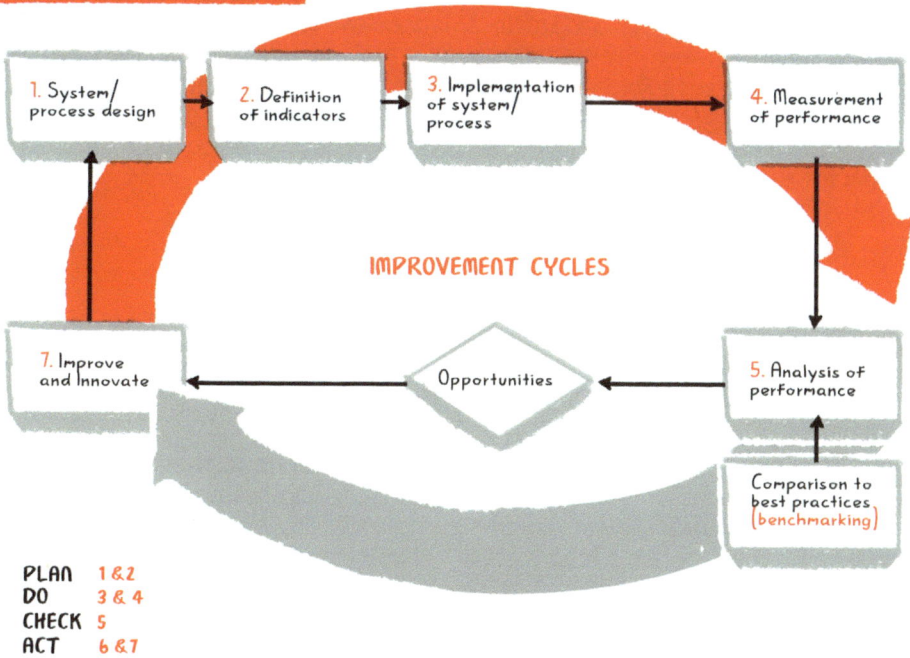

IMPROVEMENT CYCLES

1. System/ process design → 2. Definition of indicators → 3. Implementation of system/ process → 4. Measurement of performance

7. Improve and Innovate ← Opportunities ← 5. Analysis of performance

Comparison to best practices (benchmarking)

PLAN 1 & 2
DO   3 & 4
CHECK 5
ACT   6 & 7

In chapters 2 and 3, you will learn strategic and tactical tools to be used in the different steps of the PDCA - Cycles.

Maturity Levels

The maturity level of a company defines how leaders are creating, developing and maintaining a *Lean Six Sigma Management System* to produce results depending in how fast the employees learn and use methodologies and tools, and therefore a *Lean Six Sigma Management* culture is created.

It is important to know what level the company is at in order to define the right steps for a successful implementation.

> **Level 1: Start**/Traditional companies (not lean)
> **Level 2: Development**/Introduction (first lean steps)
> **Level 3: Reliable**/Growth mode
> **Level 4: Competent**/Mature mode
> **Level 5: World-class**/Excellence mode

1. **Start:** This could be a company that has just been formed, has defined all their processes, designed their products and systems, defined their key performance indicators, and is implementing everything. It could be a company that has a long history in business, but has not implemented Lean Six Sigma. Traditional companies usually don't know much about the Lean Six Sigma Philosophy. Perhaps someone did hear about it, but there is no real understanding of it. There is no formal practice of the methodology and tools for problem solving, prevention, improvement, or innovation. Normally, there are great opportunities in terms of potential results, and there is no change in structure or mindset for continuous improvement.

2. **Development:** This is a company that has started implementing Lean Six Sigma Management Tools. There has been an initial training of key members of the company. Now, Lean Six Sigma philosophy, methodology, and tools are at least known at management levels. Some initiatives and pilot projects have begun, and some good results are showing that Lean Six Sigma is a powerful strategy. They started to make Adaptation Cycles using tools to solve and prevent problems.

3. **Reliable:** This company is in the growth mode of implementation and adoption of a Lean Six Sigma culture. Companies in the Reliable step are those that are constantly measuring and analyzing their performance and continually developing corrective, preventive, improvement, and some innovation actions. Results show that every time more processes are covered within the company, the more company-wide results improve and the more motivated and enthusiastic employees from all areas are participating. The continuous improvement and Innovation Cycles are more common, and there is a commitment from more than half of employees who are moving in the right direction.

4. **Competent:** This level is a company who has defined most processes, has a clear strategy, and the strategic planning has been executed in the operational plan. At this level, most of the people in the organization practice Lean Six Sigma Philosophy, methodology, and tools. It is very common to utilize improvement and Innovation Cycles with some Adaptation Cycles.

5. **World-class:** The company has become the benchmark for the industry, customers are delighted and results show that the company has a competitive advantage among their competitors. At this level, this is a truly Lean Six Sigma Company!

The Lean Six Sigma Company - Transformation Model

Imagine a management system that generates initiative among everyone in the company to adapt to change, which keeps the whole organization in motion. The concept of "Lean Six Sigma Company" will involve all areas and all levels of an organization. It has a "Strategic" component with a set of tools that supports the *Lean Six Sigma Management System* covered in chapter 2 and a "Tactical" part supported by a tool box. This is going to be covered in chapter 3.

This book will help you understand how to move from a traditional culture to a successful Lean Six Sigma culture. Normally, we have seen the main focus in the practice of training and implementing Lean Six Sigma in the tactical part, but the strategic part is either incomplete or absent. This is one of the major reasons that Lean Six Sigma transformations fail.

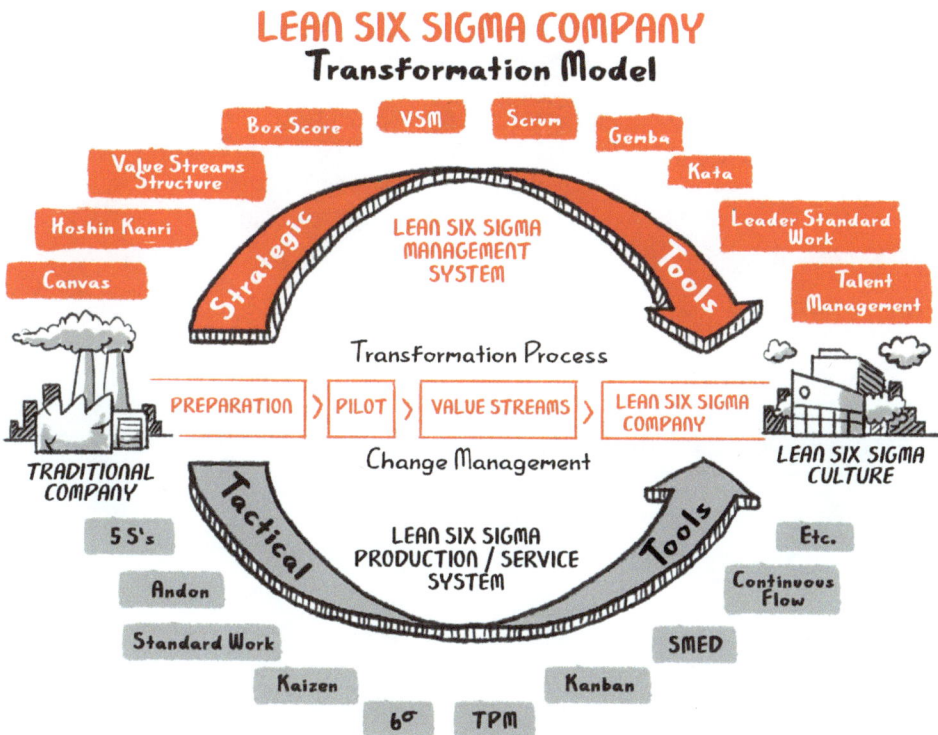

LEAN SIX SIGMA COMPANY
Transformation Model

Lean Six Sigma Management System: "The missing link"

Most organizations committed to implement a Lean Six Sigma Philosophy are missing a key ingredient: The *Lean Six Sigma Management* as a whole system, which combines the common tactical tools with a set of strategic tools. The transformation process will guide you through the phases of Preparation, Pilot, Value Streams and finally reaching the Lean Six Sigma Company and Culture phase.

In chapter 4, we will explain the Transformation Process in more detail

Lean Six Sigma Company System should include all processes, not only manufacturing or operations.

As you can see in the next graph, Lean Six Sigma Company is extended to all company processes, not just to manufacturing as many managers think. A systemic approach is required to develop agile companies because all elements need to work collaboratively to satisfy external and internal customers, and therefore, maximize the people´s and company´s potential.

Lean Six Sigma Company can be implemented in all types of businesses such as service organizations and manufacturers of any type and size.

One of our clients once said that being a Lean Six Sigma Company is the way his company should have been designed and now thanks to the knowledge and experience accumulated, everyone has it at their fingertips.

Normally there is a certification for those employees that receive training in Lean Six Sigma and demonstrate their proficiency with one or two improvement projects. But, it is important to consider that obtaining a company certification to ensure that everybody is aware of the opportunities and the level of development as a company.

More information about Lean Six Sigma Company certification will be presented in chapter 4.

In the *LSSM – Fieldbook*, we have included different assessments that you can perform in your company in order to measure where you are today in regards to the Lean Six Sigma Maturity level.

LEAN SIX SIGMA COMPANY

STRATEGIC TOOLS

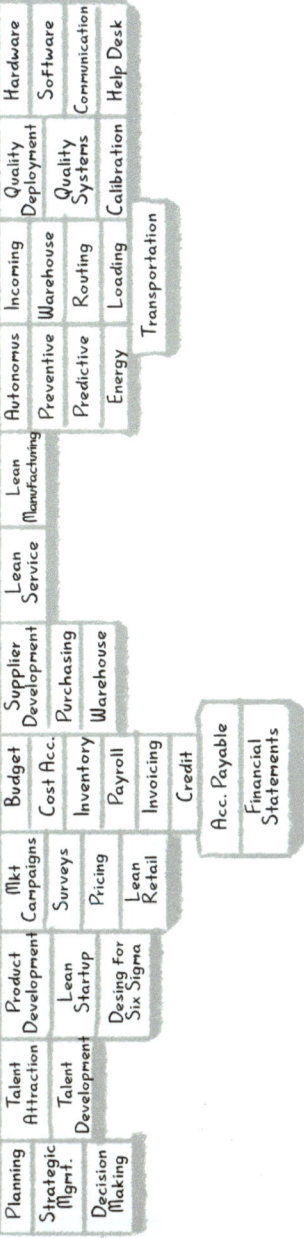

Top Mgmt.	Human Resources	Research & Develop.	Sales & Mkt	Accounting & Finance	Procurement	Service	Manufact.	Maintenance	Logistics	Quality	IT

TACTICAL TOOLS

Top Mgmt.	Human Resources	Research & Develop.	Sales & Mkt	Accounting & Finance	Procurement	Service	Manufact.	Maintenance	Logistics	Quality	IT
Planning	Talent Attraction	Product Development	Mkt Campaigns	Budget	Supplier Development	Lean Service	Lean Manufacturing	Autonomus	Incoming	Quality Deployment	Hardware
Strategic Mgmt.	Talent Development	Lean Startup	Surveys	Cost Acc.	Purchasing			Preventive	Warehouse	Quality Systems	Software
Decision Making		Desing for Six Sigma	Pricing	Inventory	Warehouse			Predictive	Routing	Calibration	Communication
			Lean Retail	Payroll				Energy	Loading		Help Desk
				Invoicing					Transportation		
				Credit							
				Acc. Payable							
				Financial Statements							

STRATEGIC TOOLS
Hoshin Kanri
Value Stream Structure
Talent Development
Agile Project Management
Standard Work for Leaders
Kata
Gemba Walks

TACTICAL TOOLS
5 S
Visual Management (Andon)
Standard Work
Personal Management

LEAN | SIX SIGMA

DMAIC

Tool set

1.3 PRINCIPLES ON WHICH THE CULTURE IS BASED

Toyota Production System – TPS has demonstrated its success because it is based on the four main principles in *The Toyota Way* book by Jeffrey Liker. The principles are essential for a Lean Six Sigma Journey and Transformation.

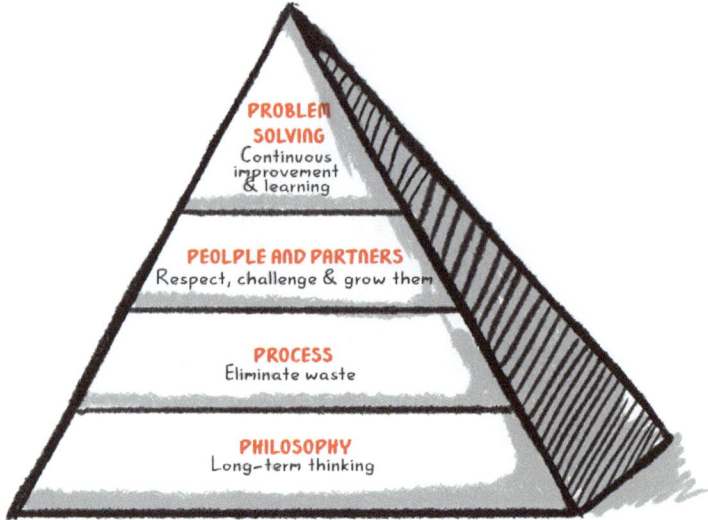

1. **Philosophy:** At the fundamental level, leaders conceive the company as a means to add value to customers, employees, society, and owners. Decisions should be made on the basis of long term philosophy even at the expense of short term financial results.
2. **Process:** The right process will produce the right results. This is why this book is going to explain the tools required to develop highly efficient and productive companies by eliminating all forms of waste, implementing a pull system to avoid overproduction, leveling the work, building a culture to stop the work and fix problems from the root cause, standardizing the work as a foundation for continuous improvement, using visual systems to prevent problems from being hidden, and only using reliable technology to help employees and processes.
3. **People and Partners:** Select and develop leaders who truly understand the work, live the philosophy, and teach others. Develop teams with members who really follow the company's philosophy and respect partners and suppliers by challenging them to new levels of performance and helping them to succeed by teaching them and developing improvements in the entire supply chain.
4. **Problem Solving:** Going to the place where things happen (Gemba) instead of in the meeting room, so everybody understands the situation, makes decisions slowly and with a consensus so that we can have a systemic approach, implements solutions rapidly, and finally becomes a learning organization through reflection and continuous improvement.

1.4 WHAT IS LEAN SIX SIGMA AND WHAT ARE THE MYTHS ABOUT IT?

In simple terms, here is the definition of some of the main terms:

- **Lean = Speed** (tools and methods to increase speed in your processes)
- **Six Sigma = Quality** (statistical process to increase quality)
- **Lean Six Sigma** (the combination is the ideal to increase speed and quality to make any process more agile, productive, and profitable)
- **Lean Six Sigma Management System** (a solid and company-wide integrated Lean Six Sigma Management System for the whole company)

Lean Manufacturing and Services

For several years, Dr. James P. Womack and colleagues at the Massachusetts Institute of Technology (MIT) conducted various studies on the automotive industry to raise awareness of the genome of the culture of quality behind the tools and thus develop healthy and agile enterprises by eliminating waste. The study was conducted to compare the best working practices in the United States with Japan and other countries to understand the differences, similarities, and especially, the factors of success and failure for companies wishing to implement them.

Lean is a philosophy of work and long-term thinking to delight customers and achieve sustained profitability. It is based on collaborative work and staff development by using tools to implement continuous improvement in order to develop stable, flexible, and continuous flow processes to provide to customers with what they need, when they need it, not before or after. It can be defined as a continuous and systematic process of identification and elimination of waste or excess, meaning any activity that does not add value in the process, but adds cost and labor.

Six Sigma

It is a business philosophy focused on customer satisfaction. It uses a methodology that reduces waste by reducing variation in processes through statistical and administrative tools, and thus significantly improves the quality in any process.

Six Sigma was developed by Motorola in the late 1980's, given the need to match or outperform their Japanese competitors, who had achieved four sigma level of quality (99% good products), when the average industry could only achieve three sigma level (93% good products). In fact, we are not speaking of defects per hundred, but defects per million.

Sigma is a Greek word (σ) that statistically measures variation. Six Sigma is based on the DMAIC methodology, which consists of improvement projects using the following steps:

- **Define:** the problem, the value for the customer, the team and the project
- **Measure:** performance, map the process, and determine the reliability of the data
- **Analyze:** identify sources of variation and root causes
- **Improve:** make changes to better performance
- **Control:** establish controls to maintain improvements made

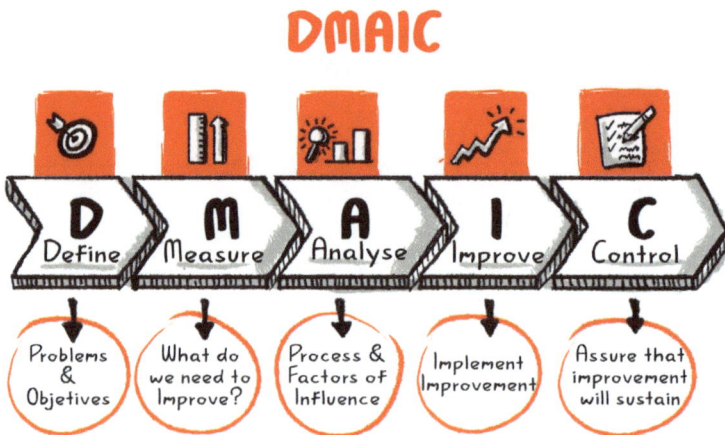

Lean Six Sigma combined is a powerful philosophy, methodology, and tool set that integrates high value knowledge generated in the history of improvement, making it a highly effective and simple system to design and manage for any type and size of company, taking into account each key organizational role: from the process of designing the plan, the product, marketing, logistics, manufacturing, services, administrative support, accounting, quality, information systems, engineering, and maintenance.

Applications of Lean Six Sigma in different industries

Lean Six Sigma can provide a significant competitive advantage and is becoming one of the most important initiatives and strategies for companies that are achieving breakthroughs.

Lean Six Sigma philosophy is applicable to virtually any industry, for example: Agriculture, Automotive, Construction, Hotels, Mining, Healthcare, Military, Startups, Education, Government, Aerospace, Banks, Restaurants, Hotels, Consulting, and many more.

Myths of Lean Six Sigma

- Six Sigma is the same as TQM
- Six Sigma is too statistical for transactional processes; it should only be used in manufacturing
- Six Sigma projects take too long to complete
- Lean Six Sigma is too complicated for our business
- Lean Six Sigma is for production only, not for engineering, or service
- Lean Sigma is for production improvement, not for process/product development
- Lean Six Sigma is not for Research and Development as it limits creativity
- A Zero-Defect Program is greater/better than Lean Six Sigma because it generates no defects while Six Sigma generates defects at 3-4 ppm
- Lean Six Sigma only costs money and will make the margins smaller
- Lean Six Sigma is a Japanese/American tool that doesn't work in Europe

Obviously, you will be confronted with myths from different people all the time. It is important that you know the concept and you can respond adequately.

Sometimes, we have had myth discussions going on and on until just before the implementation of a Lean Six Sigma improvement project. Once the project went live and employees saw what was in it for them and for the company, the myths started to disappear. Just be aware of them and be ready to respond.

1.5 THEORY OF CONSTRAINTS (TOC)

Lean Six Sigma should be implemented focusing on the main constraints. This is why we refer to the Theory of Constraints as one of the key elements on which to focus in order to achieve great results in record time.

Many companies have been implementing improvement systems, but only a few of them have succeeded because of their clear vision, focus, dedication, and persistence. The Theory of Constraints helps achieve long term results by focusing on the main constraint or bottleneck and helps companies understand where to concentrate improvement efforts in a systemic approach.

TOC was developed in the 1980's by Dr. Eliyahu M. Goldratt and is described in his best seller book: The Goal, in which he explains how to develop a management philosophy to establish priorities and work in the areas or activities that enable the organization to reach its maximum potential. Developing Lean Companies allows business goals to be achieved by applying solutions to the constraints that limits its performance. This is why the Theory of Constraints is so important to transform the culture. A constraint is any aspect that limits a system from achieving better performance with respect to its goal.

Companies are more productive only when they:
- Increase sales or throughput
- Reduce inventories
- Decrease operating expenses

Key points for theory of constraints
- Because it is a constraint, it determines the rhythm of the processes
- An hour lost in the bottleneck is an hour lost in the entire system
- Trying to make sure no resource is idle, that's a big generation of waste

Types of constraints
- Physical: people, machines, warehouse size, etc.
- Nonphysical: market demand, procedures, politics, way of thinking, etc.

What type of results can be obtained when we use **Lean Six Sigma and the Theory of Constraints** to focus on the most critical elements of a system? Data collected from 82 companies, including large companies such as Boeing and General Motors, military organizations such as the U.S. Air Force, and service companies showed the following results:

50% reduction in delivery time   *44% improvement in on time delivery*
49% reduction in inventory   *63% increase in sales (throughput)*
40% increase in net profits

These are amazing improvements and in the rest of the book, we will assume that everything we improve will be based on eliminating the main constraints.

1.6 WASTE (MUDA) AND THE HIDDEN FACTORY

Lean Six Sigma Management is an operational system that achieves great results as long as we are able to identify and eliminate all waste in every process of the value stream. This chapter is particularly important as we begin to explain how to comprehensively look for waste or limits to productivity in every phase and area of the company.

BEFORE

AFTER

J. Masini

In many companies, implementing lean is about looking for waste in manufacturing only, but we have found that sometimes, the main limitations of a company are support processes, such as marketing, product design, finance, maintenance, and service, among others. The *Lean Six Sigma Management System* can be synthesized in the sustainable elimination or minimization of three types of enemies of productivity in any area of the company:

I.Overburden   **II.Waste**   **III.Variability**

I.Overburden
Business productivity is reduced when we require people or machines to do something beyond their capabilities. We will find overburden generally in:

People. When we demand more than their capabilities or when we make them work beyond their attention and strength. Indeed, we found many cases of people working more than 12 hours consistently, with a lot of stress to deliver results, too many meetings that limit the time in which they could add value, and a hostile environment for survival in going to work that resembles going to war with unsafe conditions, heavy or dirty work, etc. The companies with high rates of overburdened employees become toxic for those who work there.

Equipment. When we force equipment, such as machinery, vehicles, computer equipment, etc., to work at a greater capacity than is recommended, under conditions of insufficient maintenance and inadequate materials or fuels. With this, we make the useful life of the equipment diminish or become a source of accidents and risks.

Suppliers. When we require them to work beyond their capabilities and limitations without respecting them.

If we are able to build a working system that generates an environment of continuous challenges in which it is a pleasure to go to work, we are really contributing to a better society and transcendence in the life of the employees.

II.Waste (Muda)

Muda is a Japanese word meaning waste or non-value-added, for which nobody wants to pay. Waste or Muda reduction is an effective way to increase profitability.

From a customer's point of view, value-added work is a process that adds value by producing goods or providing a service for which a customer is willing to pay. However, Muda is any process that consumes more resources than needed, which causes waste to occur. Waste reduces productivity, so, if we are able to recognize and eliminate waste, we immediately achieve higher levels of productivity.

One of the main objectives of Lean Six Sigma Company is to know, detect, and systematically eliminate all waste from each process of the company, since every day waste continues reduces capacity and represents a challenge for administrators, managers and employees in general.

To understand what waste is, it is convenient to first explain the activities that add value (VA). These refer to those activities that directly produce a good or service for which the customer is willing to pay. Waste or excess would be any other effort carried out in the company that is not absolutely essential to add value to the product or service, as required by the customer. These increase costs and decrease the level of service, thus affecting business results.

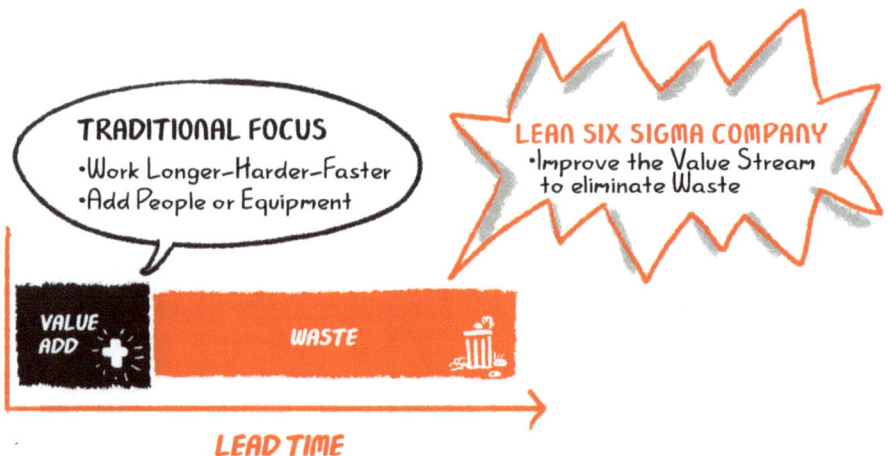

TRADITIONAL FOCUS
•Work Longer–Harder–Faster
•Add People or Equipment

LEAN SIX SIGMA COMPANY
•Improve the Value Stream to eliminate Waste

VALUE ADD

WASTE

LEAD TIME

There are 10 main types of waste

Overproduction
Basically, overproduction means:
- Produce an asset or service more than is needed or before it is needed
- To produce an asset or service faster than it is required

Excess of Inventory
It refers to any excess of materials, work in process, or finished products higher than necessary to meet the demand of the customer:
- Excess Inventory is used to cover up some of the company´s inefficiencies

Defects and Rework
These refer to the loss in the use of resources when we produce an item or defective service:
- Too many people that inspect, rework, or repair
- Inventory specifically accumulated to be reworked
- Questionable quality of the product or service
- Little interaction between customer and suppliers

Unnecessary Movements
These refer to people moving from one point to another in the workplace or in the entire company beyond what is necessary to bring value to the product, unless this movement contributes to the transformation or benefit to the customer:
- Employees walking around finding materials
- Employees walking around finding people
- Employees walking around finding tools
- Employees walking around finding documents and necessary information

Unnecessary Activities
Extra work that is unnecessary to provide value or is not required by the standards:
- Apparent existence of several bottlenecks in the process
- Lack of clear specifications from the customer
- Excess of inspections or verifications

Waits and Searches
These refer to lost time while we wait for instructions, documents, materials, tools, etc. or when we realize a task requires us to search for something:
- The operator waits for the machine to finish its processing cycle
- The machine waits for the operator to end its cycle
- Time to start a service or production

Transport of Materials and Tools
All movements of materials that do not directly support the service or production:
- Excess of handling equipment or material on forklifts
- Long conveyor belts, ramps, or pipelines
- Too many storage locations

Waste of Talent
Knowledge and experience of people as well as creativity and innovative ideas that are not shared or used:
- Staff does not feel taken into account
- Insecurity to propose new ideas
- Little or no improvement suggestions per person per year
- Environment of instability and high turnover of people

Waste of Energy
It is very common for companies to waste energy and not even realize it. Energy is often a fluid that is transformed into work such as gas or fuel, as well as electricity:
- Many air leaks in the plant
- Improper installation of the machines, wiring, networking, and so on
- Improper start of each equipment

Pollution
- Generation of hazardous waste without proper control
- Emissions that pollute the air
- Water pollution with improper or no treatment
- Emission of dust pollutants

Do you measure waste in your company?

III.Variability
Total variability of any process is the result of the variation caused by machines, materials, people, methods, etc. All of them combined result in a variation of time, quality, as well as other factors. Variability is one of the worst productivity enemies because it's not easy to measure since the most common measurement is the mean instead of the variability. Think of the many indicators your company calculates, such as mean in sales, mean in delivery time, mean in cost, etc. However, having a mean of 4 days of delivery time means that sometimes you deliver in 7 days and other days, you deliver in one day. In that case, the mean is the wrong number.

Thus, it is very important to understand the components of the variation. Six Sigma was developed with the purpose of measuring variation and understanding their various components that when combined give the total variation output. If we are able to control the variation of the different inputs (people, machines, materials, etc.), then the output result will be better (delivery on time, reaching the target cost, achieving the expected quality, etc.).

This can be: $Y = f(x)$
Where Y is the result desired from a process; i.e. high-quality level or target cost. And x represents any combination of inputs; i.e. machines, manpower or material.

What is a "Hidden Company"?

These are activities that reduce the quality or efficiency of a manufacturing operation or business process, but are not initially visible to managers; they are hidden to those seeking to improve the process.

Lean Six Sigma initiatives focus on identifying the "Hidden Company" activities in order to eliminate sources of waste and errors. As shown by the graph below, inventory usually covers many inefficiencies in the company-wide processes. When you start reducing them, the ineffectiveness will show up revealing what needs to be corrected. Hidden means because they are not visible unless you start carefully looking for them.

The "Hidden Company" requires full awareness by management when working on reduction of non-value-added activities in the manufacturing area as well as all other areas in the company.

THE SEA OF INVENTORY

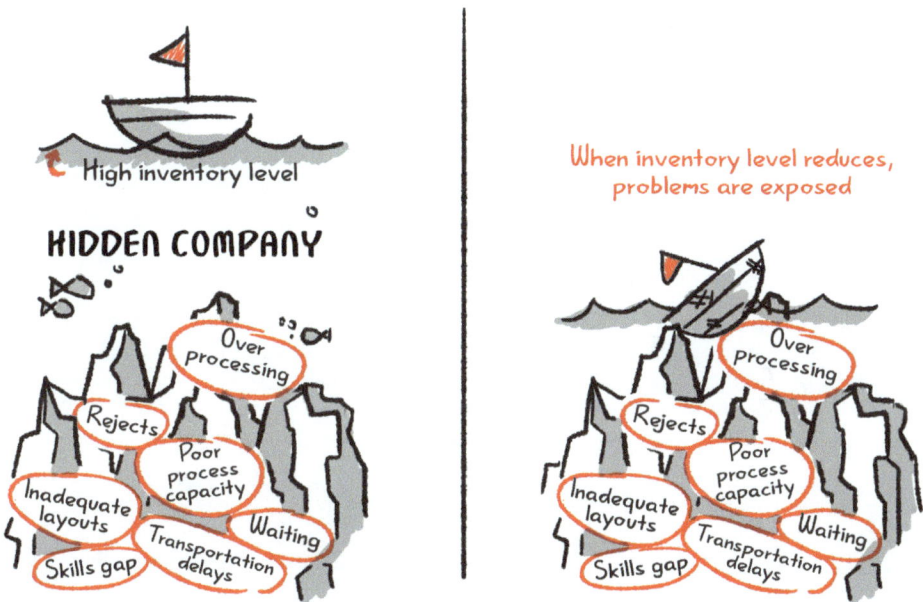

Management must make sure that Lean Six Sigma is not only a manufacturing improvement plan, but an all-encompassing and complete Lean Six Sigma philosophy that should start as early as the innovation process until the very last process, receipt of customer payments, and includes all employees of the company, all hierarchies as well as customers and suppliers.

1.7 INDUSTRY 4.0 / INDUSTRIAL INTERNET OF THINGS IIoT

The European manufacturing Industry has set a new course for its high-tech companies. Under Strategy "Industry 4.0", Germany is in transition to the 4th Industrial Revolution. Cloud computing, Internet of Things, cloud based services, big data analytics, robotics, artificial intelligence, 3-D Printing, etc. are foreseen to revolutionize how we make things/products and deliver services today and tomorrow. Our factories and businesses are changing at a fast pace; only those companies who understand and adjust their Business Model will succeed. In Parallel MIT, the Massachusetts Institute of Technologies has been working on the Industrial Internet of Things (IIoT) in order to support and guide American companies towards the digital age.

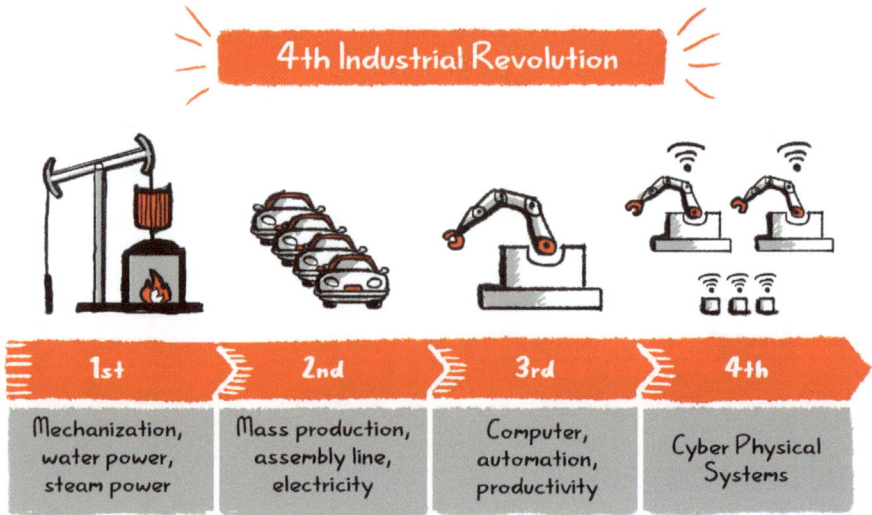

1st	2nd	3rd	4th
Mechanization, water power, steam power	Mass production, assembly line, electricity	Computer, automation, productivity	Cyber Physical Systems

The 4th Revolution is moving quickly ahead, and the basic question is: does Lean Six Sigma support Industry 4.0 / Industrial Internet of Things (IIoT) or not? Are the two principles very different and not synergistic?

Lean Six Sigma will not fade with Industry 4.0; quite the opposite actually. A solid and strong Lean Six Sigma System with stable processes is going to become even more important. The 4th industrial revolution can enable the true Lean Six Sigma Company.

Reducing waste in the form of machine breakdowns or non-value adding activities will remain fundamental. At the same time, advancements in data collection, sensors, robotics and automation, new technologies and increased computing power will enable advanced analytics and give established methods new edges. In order to trigger and benefit from all these technological innovations, what is needed are processes and companies that have a solid implementation of Lean Six Sigma. One of the most promising advances in technology is the possibility to share and act on real time information in a coordinated end-to-end supply chain. This enables a radically improved system for a just-in-time pull production. Industry 4.0 also permits a much richer understanding of the customer demand and allows the immediate sharing of data. Staying profitable and competitive in today's global business environment requires continuous improvement in productivity, quality, agility, and service levels. This pressure will only increase.

Elements of Industry 4.0
- *Autonomous* robots to help in repetitive and precision activities
- *Simulation* to visualize different options to make the best decisions
- *Internet of Things* to communicate, connect and automate decisions
- *Integration* to make systems interact with all type of databases in the cloud
- *Cybersecurity* to make all systems reliably work in the cloud
- *Cloud Computing* to make all types of system available anywhere
- *Additive Manufacturing to* produce products or parts in small quantities
- *Augmented Reality* technology that superimposes a computer-generated image on a user's view of the real world, thus providing a composite view
- *Big Data* is a large data set that may be analyzed computationally to reveal patterns, trends, and associations

Requirements
- Both Industry 4.0 / Industrial Internet of Things (IIoT) and *Lean Six Sigma Management System* need to be led by top management, not just by the IT department or by the Lean Manager
- Both need to be included in the Vision, Mission, Values, and Strategy
- Both technology and people are critical
- Both require transformational and holistic thinking
- Solid Change Management is key

Benefits from Lean Six Sigma & Industry 4.0/IIoT Philosophy
- Industry 4.0 / Industrial Internet of Things (IIoT) requires firm and stable processes
- Richer and quicker information from customer demands and deviations will result in less inventories and quicker customer response
- Much quicker one-piece flow
- Just-in-time pull production
- Radically reduced inventories
- Improved predictive maintenance (TPM) and higher OEE
- Large synergies in Lean & Digital

In recent years, we have successfully supported companies in Lean Six Sigma transformation, while they were also in transition implementing new technologies in Industry 4,0/IIoT, and we have seen that there are large synergies and benefits for higher productivity gains than without a Lean Six Sigma Philosophy. Together they can easily improve productivity by 30 - 50% in any industry.

1.8 BENEFITS OF IMPLEMENTING A LEAN SIX SIGMA MANAGEMENT SYSTEM IN YOUR COMPANY

We have examined many continuous improvement programs, and we have seen that the *Lean Six Sigma Management System* is the most powerful and effective of all, if implemented correctly. This has been proven by all the global Lean Six Sigma Transformation over the last two decades.

Benefits:
- More satisfied customers
- Improved profits
- Best Return on Investment (ROI)
- Lower investments and costs
- Committed and motivated staff
- Faster product or service delivery
- Significant reduction in inventory (RM, WIP and FG)
- Significant decrease in risks
- Client recommendations
- More competitive in the global marketplace
- Improved quality of products and services
- Reduced environmental impact
- Social impact achieved thanks to stronger economies
- Includes the whole company, from all departments to all organizational levels and processes
- Strong support for Industry 4.0 / Industrial Internet of Things (IIoT)

In chapter 5, we will explain how results are the most important components to maintain being a Lean Six Sigma Company and one of the most important strategies and initiatives the company could ever make.

1.9 LEADER'S ROLE, RESPONSIBILITIES AND KNOWLEDGE REQUIREMENTS

Before we kick of the Lean Six Sigm journey, we need to review our role and responsibilities. The leader, together with his or her key team, will be the team to get the project specified and started.

The role of the leader is to be a champion, a supporter, a guiding star. The leader will need to define the purpose, what to achieve and why, in what amount of time, and with what budget.

Company President   *Successful projects are achieved only with the full commitment of the president of the company, which means that if it is a strategy for only a division, a department, or a function of the company, it has a high risk of failure.*

Functions and Responsibilities
- Drive Lean Six Company as the most important strategy of the company
- Secure resources to achieve the successful implementation
- Design the business plan and strategy of the company
- Design the organizational structure by value streams and choose who will lead them
- Drive the talent development program as the basis for the formation of the Lean Company System and the support of all company operations
- Analyze indicators generated in the boards showing results (Box Score) and make high-level decisions to achieve fulfillment

- Provide monthly status reports of major company projects
- Change or support change of policies that prevent the company from developing its maximum potential
- Continuously monitor the processes and projects being executed
- Go for Gemba walks internally for key processes and externally with customers and suppliers

Knowledge Required
- Understanding of one's own position and industry
- Are trained as Lean managers, and in some cases, trained as Green Belts, Black Belts, or even Master Black Belts

Plant, Business Unit Vice Presidents/Directors/Managers/Chiefs
Vice presidents, directors, or managers (depending on the size of the company) will support key projects and initiatives.

Functions and Responsibilities
- Design the strategic and tactical plan of the company
- Research market conditions, global trends, and opportunities
- Find innovative strategies to achieve the goals of the company
- Design indicators to measure the company
- Propose improvement projects and resources
- Provide support for identification and selection of projects
- Guide the team that implements the projects according to the organizational strategy
- Benefit from savings and impact generated in improvement projects
- Participate in solving high level problems
- Participate in the prevention of high-level problems
- Participate in improvement projects at all levels
- Ensure resources to develop implementation of improvement events
- Provide resources and help remove barriers to project implementation
- Continuously monitor the process and ongoing projects

Knowledge Required
- Understanding of one's own position and industry
- Prepared as Lean managers and in some cases as Green Belts and Black Belts

Value Stream Leaders *Each value stream represents a family of products or services that contains the processes needed to deliver customer value.*

Functions and Responsibilities
- Have responsibility and authority for the entire value stream from when an order is received until it is delivered
- Fulfill the assigned projects of the strategic plan of the company

- Hold meetings with their process teams to assess and identify opportunities from the indicators using Lean Six Sigma methods and tools
- Analyze results of the value stream
- Propose and participate in improvement projects
- Get resources to make changes
- Provide support for identification and selection of projects
- Guide teams to implement critical projects according to the strategy of the value stream
- Benefit directly from the savings and impact generated by the improvement projects in which they participated to solve problems of the value stream
- Participate in preventing problems of the value stream
- Participate in projects to improve their value stream
- Ensure resources to develop implementation of improvement events (Kaizen)
- Provide resources and help remove barriers to project implementation
- Train team members as Green Belts and/or Black Belts

Knowledge Required
- Are prepared as Lean managers, and in some cases, as Green Belts or Black Belts

Value stream processes leaders or support leaders: Design, Marketing, Manufacturing, Service, Finance, Maintenance, etc. *They belong to a value stream, and depending on the complexity of the value stream, they may lead a team responsible for carrying out the process functions. They report to Value Stream Leader.*

Functions and Responsibilities
- Are responsible for the proper functioning of each process
- Assess and identify opportunities from the indicators in the process
- Pro-actively work to identify potential projects with colleagues
- Help define and monitor projects being executed
- Approve the project and participate in the phases required
- Participate in troubleshooting of the value stream
- Participate in preventing problems of the value stream
- Participate in projects to improve their value stream or process
- Ensure resources to develop implementation of improvement events
- Train team members as white belts and/or yellow belts

Knowledge Required
- Are prepared as Lean managers, and in some cases, as Yellow Belts or Green Belts

Partner or Operator *People who perform the service or product directly (belonging to a specific process of a value chain). They report to the leader of the process, who in turn reports to the leader of the value stream.*

Functions and Responsibilities:
- Is responsible for carrying out the operation on time and with quality
- Is thoroughly trained in his/her operation or process
- Participates in meetings at the start and end of work (methods)
- Pro-actively works to identify potential projects with their leader
- Participates in specific projects to correct, prevent, and reduce problems
- Maintains the improvements by making them part of their daily work

Knowledge Required
- Trained and understands own job description
- Prepared as White and/or Yellow Belts

External instructors/guides/implementers
Consider hiring instructors or implementation guides if you find instructors that not only teach the tools, but are willing to actively participate in the implementing change as a way of teaching the staff of the company in order to accelerate their learning, so that implementation develops at a smooth rate. Consider instructors or guides as being the ones who will actively show you the correct way to teach, implement, and negotiate internal changes as an example and not just as those who do the work for you. It is very important that your guides are willing to spend more time during the development and are dedicated to spending most of their time analyzing the improvements. They need to be part of your team, commit, and support the change process in order to achieve the goal.

Knowledge Required
- Expert in Lean Six Sigma tools
- Experience in coaching and training
- Experience in company transformation

Lean Six Sigma Training and Certification Levels
- **Lean Management**
- **White Belt**
- **Yellow Belt**
- **Green Belt**
- **Black Belt**
- **Master Black Belt**

For a Lean Six Sigma journey, every company will need to have trained and certified employees in Lean Six Sigma in all the different training levels. You might ask, why do we need to have them? This is quite an investment and takes valuable time of the employees! You are right, but consider that if you want to implement a new language spoken in your company by all employees, you will need to train the employees. If not, the effective use and implementation will not work or be guaranteed.

These trained employees in *Lean Six Sigma Management System* will understand the philosophy, will be capable of using the right tools when working together in an improvement project, speak the same language and acronyms. Once you have trained and certified the employees, you will have approximately the following distribution:

Lean Six Sigma Management System implementation can only be implemented successfully if we understand the basic philosophy, the key tools, and their benefits. Implementing Lean Six Sigma in one or another area or department of the company will have some minor benefit, but the complete benefits of a whole system cannot be achieved. Usually this type of implementation dies after a certain time.

So, what we need to do is to have some systematic training within the company. The purpose of initial training will be to align all towards the common purpose and objective.

We recommend that you first train the whole management team in basic *Lean Six Sigma Management System*, this can take up to one day. The second day would ideally be to train the whole company in White Belt, or in other words, the basic Lean Tools.

TRAINING	ABBREV.	% OF PEOPLE	KNOWLEDGE	COURSE TIME PER MODULE	ACCUMULATED TRAINING
Lean Management	LM	All leaders	Philosophy, Strategic and Tactical Tools	8 hours	8 hours
White Belt	WB	100%	Introduction and Basic Tools	8 hours	16 hours
Yellow Belt	YB	20% to 50%	Lean Methods and Tools	24 hours	40 hours
Green Belt	GB	10% to 20%	Six Sigma Methods and Tools	40 hours	80 hours
Black Belt	BB	1% to 3%	Leadership, Project Management, Lean Company	40 hours	120 hours
Master Black Belt	MBB	1 per 10 BB	Strategy Management, Inovation Tools	40 hours	160 hours

Training should also be a combination of learning and doing, in which participants from management, the implementation team, and members of the pilot process receive training.

Training must be performed by professionals to the managers and implementation teams, with the coordination and administration of the department of Human Resources of the company, which will be responsible for monitoring and sustaining the system.

Key training programs to get the teams prepared

Lean Management *(one day) for the whole management team.*
It is recommended that business owners and executives who design the future of the company receive training to meet the objective, scope, tools, process implementation, and expected results of a Lean Company.

All company executives:
- Drive Lean Company as the most important strategy of the company
- Ensure resources for implementation
- Approve critical projects for implementation of the strategic plan
- Give guidelines to value stream teams
- Remove internal political barriers
- Identify opportunities for improvement
- Know the philosophy and train people around them

The members of the management team should also be trained as Yellow Belts and Green Belts; in fact, some companies make this a requirement for management positions.

Management tools: Hoshin Kanri, Value Stream Structure, and Value Stream Mapping.

White Belt *(one day) for 100% of employees*
It is recommended that everyone in the company be trained in the basic philosophy, principles, and tools of Lean to ensure a long-term continuous improvement culture, so that they may be aware of the opportunities and participate in the implementation and maintenance of the system.

- Devote no more than 10% of their time on projects when they are part of an implementation team
- Understand and apply Lean tools and Six Sigma
- Detect application areas for potential Lean Six Sigma projects
- Provide support in implementation and monitoring of Lean Six Sigma projects
- Participate in at least two projects per year with a typical impact of 10,000 USD per year total
- Every day practice of Lean Six Sigma tools and culture

White Belt Tools: 5 S's (Housekeeping), Andon (Visual Management), Standardized Work.

Yellow Belt *(one-week training) for 20-50% of employees*
It is recommended to train 20% to 50% of all employees responsible for process improvement as Yellow Belts in a company, so that they can become experts in implementing Lean tools. They can be personnel from different areas and levels that are involved in the implementation of projects and can be assigned projects part time because of their knowledge and experience in order to achieve successful projects as part of a team.

- Devote no more than 20% of their time on projects
- Understand and apply Lean Six Sigma tools
- Detect areas for potential Lean Six Sigma projects

- Provide support in implementation and monitoring of LSS Projects
- Participate in at least two projects per year with a typical impact of 25,000 USD per year total
- Every day practice of Lean Six Sigma tools and culture
- The Yellow Belts should train around ten White Belts annually

Green Belt *(one-week training) for approximately 10% to 20% of employees*
It is recommended that key employees responsible for problem solving and improving quality be trained as Green Belts. They can be employees from different areas and levels that support Black Belts in the implementation of projects and are assigned full or part-time to projects because of their knowledge and experience in order to achieve successful projects.

- Devote no more than 20% of their time on projects when they are part of an implementation team
- Understand and apply Lean Six Sigma tools
- Help detect areas for potential Lean Six Sigma projects
- Provide support in implementation and monitoring of projects
- Participate in at least two projects per year with a typical impact of 50,000 USD per year

Black Belt *(one-week training) for 1-3% of employees*
They are leaders responsible for continuous improvement training, managing, and implementing complex projects.

They are experts in the implementation of projects and the use of Lean Six Sigma tools and are usually dedicated full-time to the implementation of projects. Main change agents within the organization to transform into a Lean Six Sigma Company.

- Give support to prioritizing potential Lean Six Sigma projects
- Lead in the development, implementation, and monitoring of Lean Six Sigma projects
- Develop at least four projects each year with a typical impact of 125,000 USD per year

They understand and practice the applications of Lean Six Sigma philosophy, methodology and tools in: Design, Logistics, Business, Manufacturing, Service, Accounting, Information technologies, Quality and Maintenance.

Personnel from value streams or areas of support within a value stream may be trained as Black Belts and perform these duties even though they do not devote 100% of their time, as their knowledge is very useful for the development of projects and sustaining results. However, it is important to keep dedicated Black Belts to train other people in the organization.

It is also recommended that Black Belts work on developing projects of improvement that take up to one and a half to two years to complete, and then they can return to the business operations to sustain the transformation and transfer the project to other Black Belts to devote to continuous improvement.

Note: It is important that if there are Black Belts in the organization, they should not be assigned activities that are routine operations because then they would not be able to perform either activity satisfactorily. This has been one of the reasons for failure of implementation at some companies.

Master Black Belt *(one-week training) for 1% of employees*
Requirements: Black Belt certified. They are subject matter experts in the Lean Six Sigma philosophy, methodology, and tools, who guide the Black Belts.

They usually spend most of their time guiding projects from a corporate and strategic perspective, guiding in achieving financial results, and are a link between leaders and managers in large companies to manage resources.

They usually report to the General Manager or senior strategic business directors as Lean Six Sigma projects are carried out in all areas of the company.

- Strategically manage the implementation of Lean Six Sigma Company
- Guide the process of strategic and tactical planning of the company and its Value Streams
- Are involved in the design of the structure by Value Streams
- Participate in the program design of talent development
- Teach methodologies and tools to managers and Black Belts
- Give direction to the Black Belts on at least ten projects a year with a typical impact of 500,000 USD a year

These specialists are acquired to the extent to which the program is implemented, and they are certified as specialists. The Master Black Belts train and guide the Black Belts. They should train about ten Black Belts annually. They also train and guide Green Belts and should also train about ten Green Belts annually. In small companies, there could be a single Black Belt who works full time for implementation when required.

Master Black Belts develop the overall direction of the Lean Six Sigma strategy of the company.

We end Chapter 1 by highlighting some Key Points. Please feel free to add points that are additionally important to you.

1.10 KEY POINTS

1. *Lean Six Sigma Management System* is a proven continuous improvement system and has been introduced successfully in companies throughout the globe.

2. *Lean Six Sigma Management System* is not just a set of tools; it's a way of life.

3. *Lean Six Sigma Management System* is not just for manufacturing and largescale corporations like GE or Motorola, but for any industry and any size company.

4. In order to implement it successfully, it will require a clear understanding, strategy, plan, dedication, discipline, and strict follow-up.

5. Management must play a key role and participate in involvement and commitment in order to implement *Lean Six Sigma Management System* and sustain it. Be aware of myths.

6. Theory of Constraints (TOC) focuses on the major constraints or bottlenecks of the system giving Lean Six Sigma Company the best chance to achieve results in record time.

7. Waste and Muda are non-value-added processes or steps for which nobody wants to pay, so must be persistently eradicated.

8. Be aware of the "Hidden Factory."

9. Becoming a True Lean Company should be the aspiration and long-term goal.

10. The implementation of Industry 4.0 / Industrial Internet of Things (IIoT) will strongly benefit from a *Lean Six Sigma Management System* Implementation.

11. There are significant benefits in implementing a *Lean Six Sigma Management System.*

12. Be aware of myths and potential roadblocks of Lean Six Sigma.

13. Prepare your company with the required skills and resources.

14. Be aware of the leader's role, responsibilities and knowledge requirements.

15. Get the right Lean Six Sigma support from outside with the right commitment and skills.

Please add your other Key Points:

_____
_____
_____
_____
_____
_____
_____
_____
_____
_____
_____
_____
_____
_____
_____
_____
_____
_____
_____
_____
_____
_____
_____
_____
_____
_____
_____
_____
_____
_____
_____
_____
_____
_____
_____

CHAPTER 2

2. STRATEGIC TOOLS

2. STRATEGIC TOOLS

Strategy is a high - level plan for how to achieve the goal

A thorough strategic plan and its execution is key for the success of any project. Many companies jump too quickly into tactical tools like 5 S's, Visual Management, SMED, TPM, etc. Without analysis, planning, or strategic thoughts. Over time, this may lead to some departmental improvements. Unfortunately, most of the time there is little or no improved bottom line results for the company. The Lean Six Sigma journey does not achieve the desired results and ends when a new boss comes on board.

We want to make the *Lean Six Sigma Management System* work sustainably, improve customer satisfaction, provide stable processes, and achieve strong bottom line results, independent of who is leading the company. The following is a set of key strategic tools we have assembled. There are more tools available, but we wanted to focus on the most common ones that leaders and companies have successfully used.

During the transformation process through our *Lean Six Sigma Management* journey, we will use strategic tools in the different steps of the PCDA – Cycle. As we talk about strategy, make sure you select the tools that will best suit your company and teams. The arrows indicate where you can use which tools within the PDCA Cycle.

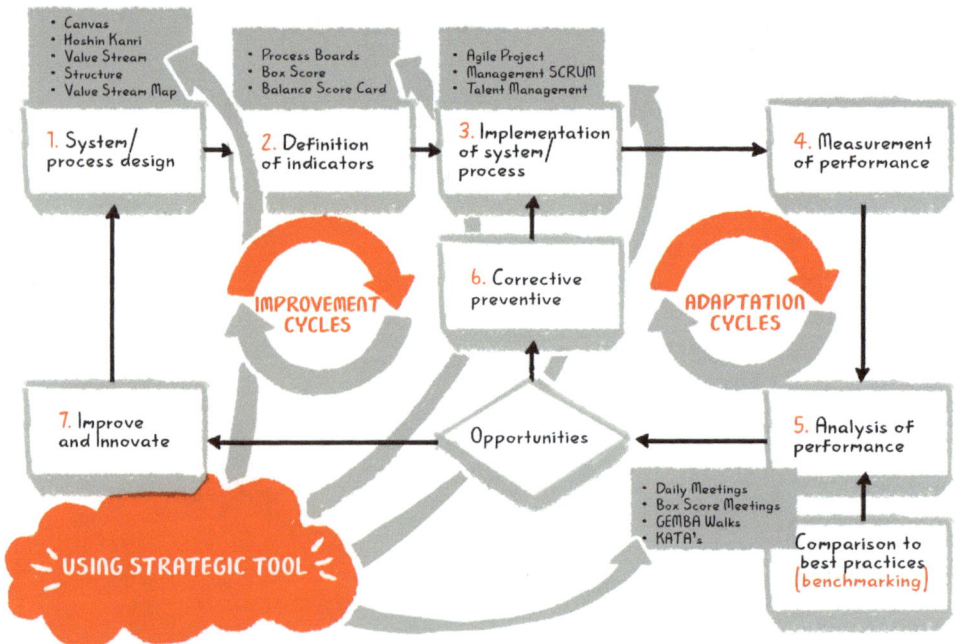

2.1 LEAN SIX SIGMA COMPANY ASSESSMENTS - MATURITY LEVELS

Let's begin with an assessment of Lean Six Sigma company. This will help you to assess the Lean Six Sigma Level of your company, plants and processes. We use a three-step approach with different assessment levels in order to measure the Lean Six Sigma Maturity of the company, of the plant and the Value Stream.

Assessments:
1. **Company Maturity Level** (CEO and Directors)
2. **Value Stream Maturity Level** (Value Stream Managers)
3. **Support Process Area Maturity Level** (Support Process Managers)

These are simple questionnaires filled out by the respective leaders and the results are from a 1 (Traditional - no lean maturity) to 5 (Excellence or world-class) as explained in Chapter 1. Depending on the level, we will develop a specific Lean Six Sigma Strategic Plan. Below are a few examples of questionnaires filled out.

These assessments will help your teams have a first-hand understanding of where you are at in a Lean Six Sigma transformation. We have found that companies and individuals usually overevaluate themselves from having been trained in using some of the tools or by the fact that some of the tools have been implemented in some areas of the company.

The key for us is: Are these tools providing a better performance, better EBITDA, or better customer satisfaction? If not, then we are sorry to say that, it is only an expense. We need to avoid doing something that is not generating value.

Once we have the assessment, we need to look at it as a team along with an experienced Master Black Belt to select the strategic tools to move forward.

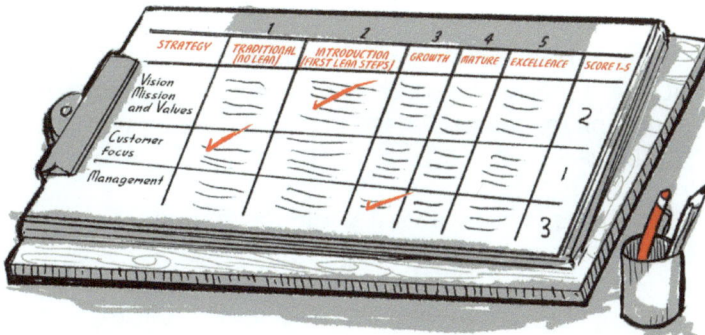

In the LSSM - Fieldbook you will find all the forms to conduct the assessment.

49

2.2 LEADERSHIP AND CHANGE MANAGEMENT

Leadership is the ability to lead or guide individuals, teams, or the entire organization to a desired destination.

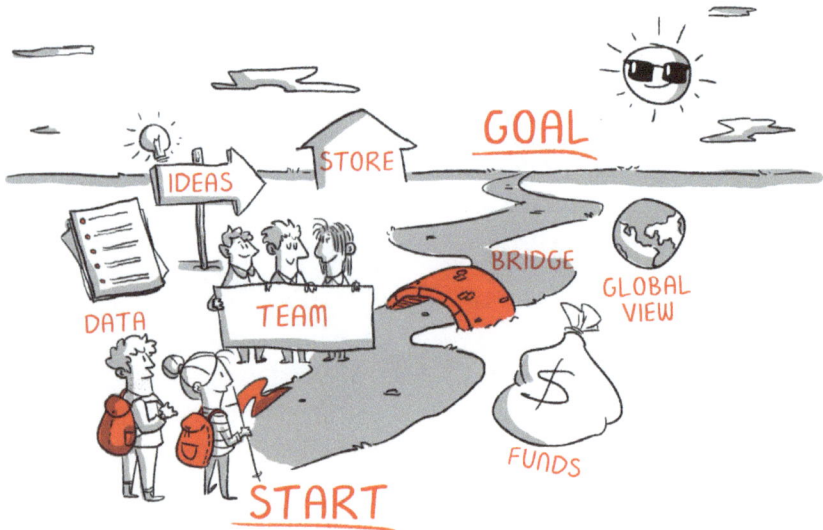

In order to be able to implement a successful *Lean Six Sigma Management System*, we need to make sure that proper leadership is in place. Let's start with what leaders and managers do. Let's be clear. Both types of personality traits are necessary in a company, and actually, a leader will incorporate both of them, depending on the situation.

Effective leaders continually ask questions, probing all levels of the organization for information, testing their own perceptions, and rechecking the facts. They want to know what is working and what is not. Leaders investigate reality, taking in the pertinent factors, and analyzing them carefully. On this basis, they produce visions, concepts, plans, and programs.

Managers adopt the truth from others and implement it without probing for the facts that reveal reality. We all know that there is a profound difference between leaders and managers. A good manager does things right – a leader does the right things.

Doing the right things implies a goal, a direction, an objective, a vision, a dream, or a path.

Management is about systems, controls, procedures, policies, and structure. Leadership is about trust — about people. A leader is someone who has the capacity to create a compelling vision that takes people to a new place and translates that vision into action. Leaders draw other people to them by enrolling them in their vision. What leaders do is inspire people and empower them.

A Leader sets his/her focus on:
- People, Talents, Vision, Mission, Values, Strategy
- What and Why
- Identifying potential
- Integrating change
- Motivation and trust
- Challenges
- Empowerment and inspiration through direct communication

A Manager sets his/her focus on:
- Systems, structures, parameters, and standards
- How and When
- Budgeting and detailed plans
- Monitoring and controlling
- Maintaining and administrating
- Problem solving and removing obstacles

Attributes of leadership that every Lean Six Sigma leader should have:
- **VISION:** Very clear image of what the company wants to become and which way to go (Creative Leadership)
- **SHARED VISION:** Imparting an understanding of the company´s philosophy and vision so that everyone makes the vision their own (Emotional Leadership)
- **EXECUTION:** Being capable of converting the plan into action while supporting everybody (Technical Leadership)
- **TEAM DEVELOPEMET:** Being able to form great teams that will be self-managed (Human Leadership)
- **ETHICAL VALUES:** Basing all decisions and actions on ethical principles (Ethic Leadership)

Change Management Process

When implementing any big change initiative like *Lean Six Sigma Management System* throughout the company, it is key to plan a successful Change Management Process. Let's be honest. People in general don't like change, and an initiative like *Lean Six Sigma Management System* can be seen as a risk for them, difficult to do, or just not the right thing to do, so they reject or resist supporting it.

Before we start any initiative, we need to adequately prepare all employees in order to make them understand the "what" we are going to do, the "why", the "when", the "whom" and the "what's in it" for the company and for themselves.

If you are at all familiar with the change curve, the images below show how the morale and productivity of everyone changes with the progress of the project. It's not a straight line. During a typical change process there is an S-Curve that people will go through. The S-Curve has different phases and will impact morale and productivity over time. We need to know and plan adequately for the different phases.

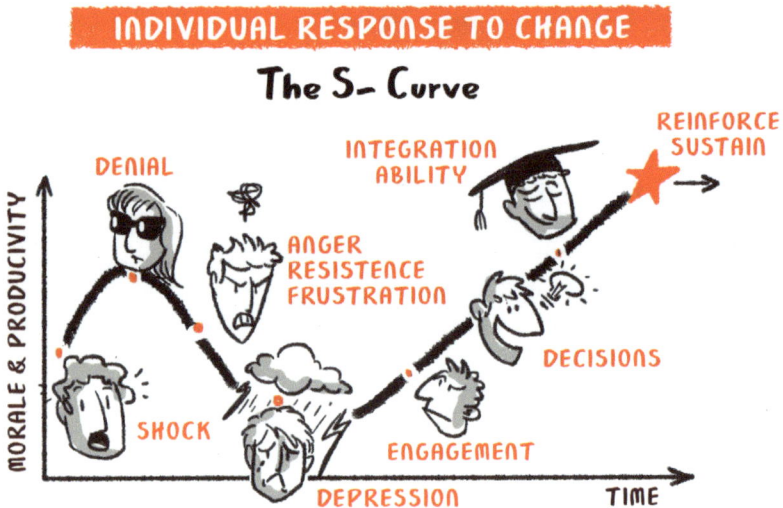

INDIVIDUAL RESPONSE TO CHANGE

The S- Curve

The phases of the S-Curve are:
- **Shock** – "Wow! This is going to impact us!"
- **Denial** – "We don't need this"
- **Anger / Resistance Frustration** – "I'm going to lose my job"
- **Depression** – "I can't deal with this"
- **Engagement** – "Hey, maybe I can deal with this"
- **Decisions** – "Hey, they are supporting me"
- **Integration Ability** – "Hey, it's better than before"
- **Reinforce Sustain** – "I support and maintain the new improved system"

We need to be very aware of these phases; neglecting or shortcutting them will lead to a rejection of the project. The larger the project, the more it will affect employees and the more you will need to invest time and focus in change curve. The leader of the company is the sponsor of the change and sets up an interdisciplinary team that will support the communication and implementation of the project.

Change Management Process Approaches
During our work in companies, we have observed many good change management processes. We greatly like two of these processes because they are simple and effective to implement.

One process that we recommend using is John Kotter's and the other one is John Van Maanen's approach.

John Kotter's very effective 8-Step Process
1. **Increase urgency:** As leaders, we need to raise a feeling of urgency, so that people start telling each other "we must do something" about the problems and opportunities in order to reduce the complacency, fear, and anger that prevent change from starting.

2. **Build a guiding team:** As leaders, we need to help pull together the right group of people with the right characteristics and sufficient power to drive the change effort while helping them to behave with trust and emotional commitment to one another.

3. **Get the vision right:** As leaders, we need to help create the right and compelling vision to direct the effort and help the guiding team develop strategies for making a bold vision a reality.

4. **Communicate for buy-in:** As leaders, we need to express very clear, credible, and heartfelt messages about the direction of change, so that all employees will understand why we are making the change and what's in it for them.

5. **Enable action:** As leaders, we need to help remove barriers that block those who have genuinely embraced the vision and strategies. By taking away sufficient obstacles in their organizations and in their hearts, they behave differently.

6. **Create Short-Term Wins:** As leaders, we need to make sure that we generate sufficient wins at a fast-enough pace to diffuse cynicism, pessimism, and skepticism.

7. **Don't let up:** Once the wheel starts to move, we need to help people create wave after wave of change until the vision is reality without allowing urgency to dissipate.

8. **Make it stick:** As leaders, we need to make sure that people continue to act in the new way, despite the pull of tradition, by establishing behaviors in a reshaped organizational culture.

John Van Maanen's Approach

John Van Maanen developed a Three-System Approach (Strategic, Political, and Cultural), and if they are all under control, then a successful execution can be achieved.

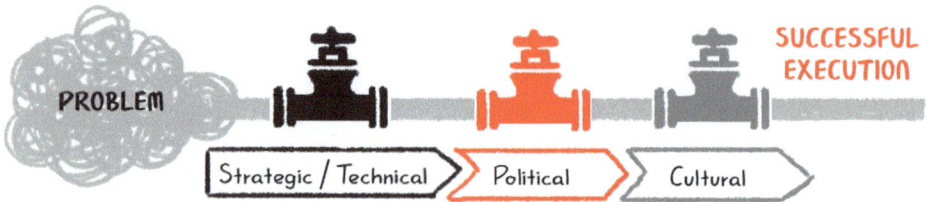

1. Strategic/Technical

- **Grouping**: Is the organization design appropriate to achieve the initiatives to insure successful implementation of Lean Six Sigma?
- **Linking:** Are the appropriate mechanisms for sharing information in place? Are more or less required? Why?
- **Alignment:** Are the appropriate performance measures, incentives, planning, and budgeting systems, etc. in place to support the current initiatives?

2. Political System

- Who are the key internal stakeholders that can influence the Lean Six Sigma implementation? What are their interests? What sources of leverage and power do they have internally and externally?
- Are the main stakeholders in this activity likely to be able to build an effective informal or formal coalition to support Lean Six Sigma implementation? What stakeholders might it involve?

3. Cultural System

- Who is engaged in or affected by the Lean Six Sigma implementation?
- What basic assumptions about your organization support the Lean Six Sigma Implementation? Which ones work against it?
- What "mental models" about the way your organization does business are challenged by the Lean Six Sigma Implementation? How deeply are they held?

Using both processes is the best you could do. We recommend setting up an interdisciplinary team to plan all the phases. Don't take short-cuts, as this will be well invested time and will make the project successful.

Communication Plan – key to any change initiative

As we mentioned previously, we recommend setting up a communication plan in the company. This will allow all stakeholders to align and buy in.

An effective plan will consist of
- What we will communicate
- Why we want to communicate
- When do we want to communicate
- Whom do we want to reach

Set up a Team
- Set up a specific communication team that will assure the effective communication to all levels and areas

What to communicate?
- Communication of the Lean Six Sigma transformation is an internal marketing campaign to inform everyone how the company will be developed to the next level with the contribution of all employees and the importance of being part of this project. Communication should be positive and always seek to support the transformation.

The management team should communicate
- Why a Lean Six Sigma company transformation is a very important journey
- Everybody is involved
- Training in different levels is key for the full understanding and commitment
- Phases of the implementation: Preparation, Pilot, Value Stream, Company-wide
- Progress of training, activities, and achievements
- Results achieved and how these results are giving a competitive advantage

Requirements

- Make sure the content or message is simple and very clear
- Make sure you define a clear timing of the communication; set up a timetable
- Define the communication platforms (internal newspaper, intranet, meetings)
- Make sure the communication is written and that all key people will use the same message
- Make sure you know your stakeholders and you get them on board early
- Prepare ahead a Q & A summary and have common answers
- Pretest the communication plan with a small group
- After an initial communication, set up some workshops for Q & A
- Explain what's in it for the company and what's in it for each employee

Do's

- Be clear and honest
- Describe the consequences if the change isn't implemented
- Discuss how employees will be helped through the change
- Follow the plan
- Be close to your employees; they will have questions and want answers from you
- Do a weekly review of what communication went well and what needs to be improved
- If people don't support the initiative and even sabotage actions, you need to take immediate action

During your last big initiative, did you have an effective communication plan in place? Did you fail or could it have been better?

In the LSSM – Fieldbook, there is a ready to use format for change management and an effective communication plan.

2.3 VALUE PROPOSITION - CANVAS

Leaders from all types of companies around the world are facing important challenges on how to design the way their companies should run and what type of decisions they need to make in an environment of high uncertainty. Strategic conversations are normally not very productive due to a limited knowledge and understanding of the key elements of a business.

Business model design is very important for companies so that even when they have extraordinary products, if the business model is not correctly designed, it can result in future failure. For example, when Xerox created a very fast copy machine that was very expensive, only a few customers bought it. It was only when they redesigned the business model to lease the machines that the company generated great financial rewards.

Every company, from new to old, needs to regularly review their business model in order to understand the way they create and deliver value to their customers.

Business Model called Canvas

A business model is a map of how the business is going to create and deliver value to their customers and how it is intended to generate revenue and profits. The Canvas Business Model was developed by Alexander Osterwalder as a PhD thesis with Yves Pigneur as his doctoral mentor.

The Canvas Business Model is a graphical tool used to describe what value is offered to clients, how this value is created, the way this value is communicated (channels) and delivered, the way the customers understand the current business model, and then creates the future model to achieve the company's objectives.

CANVAS MODEL

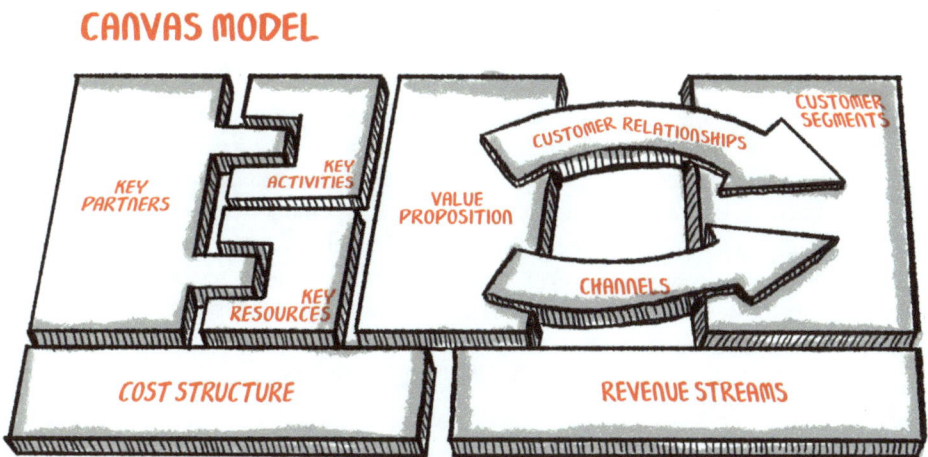

Elements of a Canvas Business Model:

1. **Customer Segments:** Different groups of clients with similar characteristics and needs to be covered by the value proposition.
2. **Value Proposition:** The way the product or service solves problems or satisfies needs.
3. **Channels:** The way you communicate and deliver the value proposition to your clients.
4. **Customer Relationships:** The way you establish and maintain relations with each customer segment.
5. **Revenue Streams:** The monetary result of every value proposition.
6. **Key Resources:** The critical means necessary to offer the elements previously described.
7. **Key Activities:** Critical processes or activities necessary to develop value to the customers.
8. **Key Associations:** People or companies that provide activities or supplies to the system.

The Canvas Business Model is being taught by the best universities in the world, such as Harvard and Stanford, as well as at Osterwalder workshops. Canvas exercises are led by top managers and generally guided by experienced Master Black Belts who lead the teams in the use and development of Canvas to generate dynamic and productive exercises of creating and debugging business models to ensure good results.

It is important that people from all different areas such as designers, sales and marketing people, accountants, process engineers, purchasing, human resources, etc. participate in the generation of new ideas, debugging them and ensure the correct implementation of the selected models.

In 1958, Xerox invented a copy machine that could make 2,000 copies a day when the competition could make only 30 to 40 copies. The machine was seven times more expensive, so sales where not what expected. They had a great product but a terrible business model. They did a market study and concluded that no customer would buy such an expensive machine. But when they re-designed the business model to be based on an annuity model with leasing the machine, that resulted in significant recurring revenue and cash generation. In 2011, approximately, 83 percent of their total revenue was annuity-based revenue that included contracted services, equipment maintenance, consumable supplies, financing, among other elements. The company reinvented their business and became very successful.

As you see from this example, the right business model can make the difference between being the best or the last even with a great product or service.

In the LSSM – Fieldbook you can work through a CANVAS example and you will have the opportunity to practice to develop your own CANVAS business model for your company, business unit, or startup business.

2.4 LEAN STRATEGY, VISION AND TARGET DEPLOYMENT WITH HOSHIN KANRI

Once we have worked out or reviewed the Business Model, the strategy is the next step to review. The strategy is the game plan and provides a clear focus for the company in order to succeed in the marketplace and to distinguish you from your competitors. The Canvas model can be used to make the options visible, now we need to focus on the plan. As Roger L. Martin explained:
"People make strategy much harder than it needs to be. For some it is that they focus too much on tools like SWOT analysis, customers analysis, competitor analysis, financial modeling, and so on. Others thinks that strategy is all about changing direction". Yes, we will need analysis, but more important, we need to make decisions.

The approach is basically to answer the following five questions:

1. What are the broad **aspirations** for the organization and **the concrete goals** against which we can measure our progress?
2. Across the potential fields available to us, **where** will we choose **to play and not to play?** Be very clear; the more focused, the more chances there are to be better than competition.
3. In our chosen place to play, **how** will we choose **to win** against our competitors?
4. What **capabilities** are necessary **to build** and maintain to win in our chosen field?
5. **What management system** is necessary **to operate** to build and maintain the key capabilities?

Use the strategy wheel below developed by Harvard Business School in order to answer the above questions for each department of your company. The purpose in the middle of the wheel is your Vision – Mission - Purpose of your company. It's all about aligning your functions and plans to the center.

In the LSSM – Fieldbook, you can see an example of a Strategy definition and you will have the opportunity to practice to develop your own strategy.

According to Harvard Business School, only between 10% and 20% of companies in the world make a strategic plan, 91% of executives qualify as "exceptional decision-makers", 90% of companies do not systematically execute the strategy; and 80% of people do not understand the goals of the company. In other words, it is very important that we use a tool to execute the strategy.

Hoshin Kanri is a strategic planning tool to describe the company's philosophy and deployed to specific actions to make it work by incorporating the vision into strategies, strategies into projects, and projects into actions for everyone in the company.

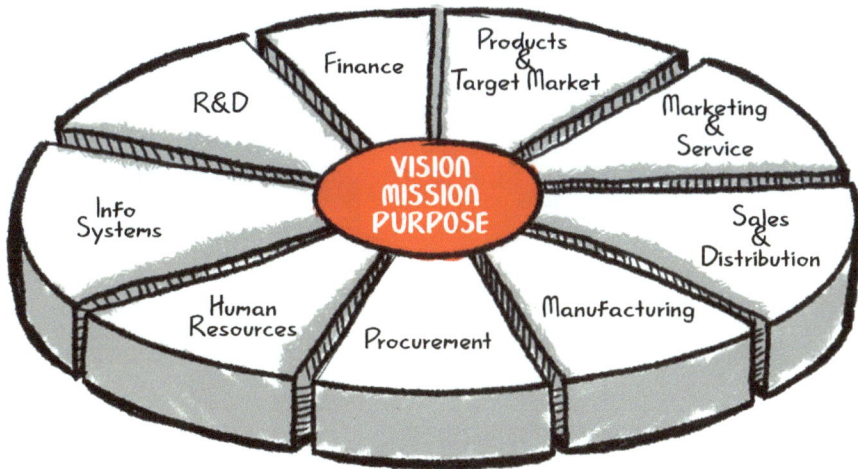

Strategic Deployment

Strategic planning is the creation of a unique value proposition involving a set of different activities. The essence of strategy is the decision to perform activities differently than rivals do.

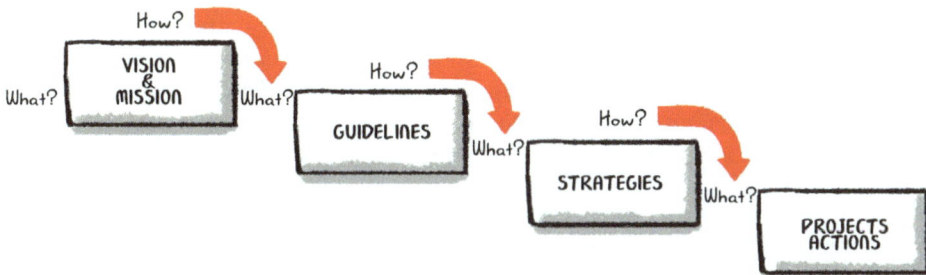

All companies need to use Hoshin Kanri. We often see the following situations that would not happen if Hoshin Kanri were used:

- Year-to-year plans never seem to connect
- Most employees never seem to feel part of the team
- Little connection between strategy and continuous improvement
- Bad projects in process
- Improvement time is too long
- Budget and forecasts are constantly not met
- The vision of senior management does not coincide with the activities of the organization
- Too many good projects in process

Hoshin Kanri is a systematic approach for identifying, ordering, and resolving activities that require drastic change or improvement.

Hoshin Kanri functions as a framework based on the cooperation of the whole company to achieve the long-term strategic objectives and the short-term management plan.

After the Second World War, some Japanese managers blended the teachings of management by objectives from Dr. Deming and Juran and developed a framework, known as Hoshin Kanri.

Japanese translation: **Hoshin** = Direction of the needle or the compass, **Kanri** = Management.

Other terms for Hoshin Kanri:

- Hoshin Planning (Hewlett-Packard)
- Policy Deployment (AT & T, Infineon Technologies)
- Policy Management (Texas Instruments)
- Performance Management (Xerox)
- Priority management
- Deployment of goals
- Process "Catch-ball"

Hoshin Kanri is an alignment tool across the entire structure of the company by setting top-down goals, translating the organization's objectives into actions based on the priorities determined by the management, aligning goals of individuals, teams, and functions with those of the organization, and finally choosing only the projects that will most help meet the business goal.

Benefits of Hoshin Kanri:
- There is a clear line of sight
- There is clear leadership at all levels
- Each employee is clear about his/her role and objectives
- Everyone understands the goals of the organization
- It aligns resources, objectives, and metrics to all goals and levels of the organization
- Employees are involved in setting goals, improvement schedules, and reviews

When used?
- Start of operations: Basic plan Hoshin Kanri and Global Box Score (1-week duration)
- Annually: Main plan update Hoshin Kanri (2-4 days)
- Monthly: Evaluation of global progress Global Box Score or Balance Scorecard (1 hour)
- Weekly: Evaluation of value chain advances of the Box Score (30 minutes)
- Daily: Evaluation of advances per hour and daily Floor Board (5 minutes)

Many of our costumers develop their own personal Hoshin Kanri, where they define financial objectives, family, personal and professional projects, etc.

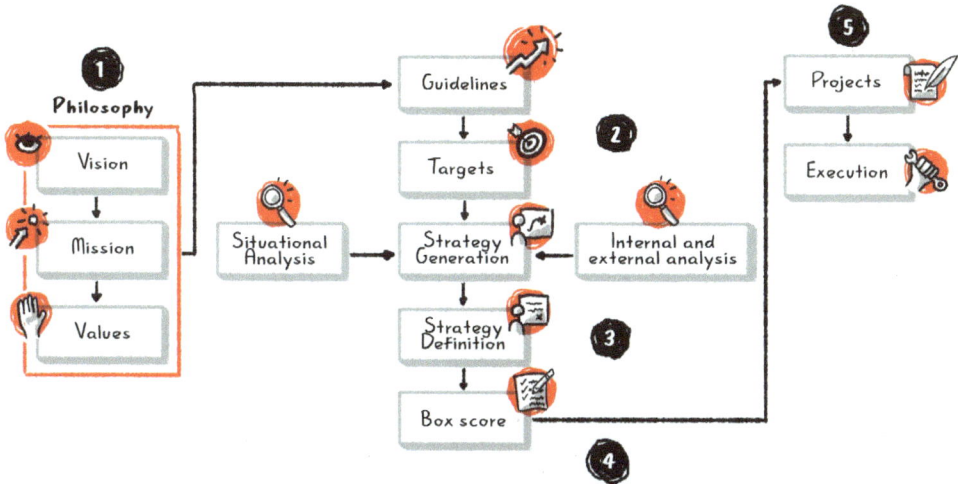

Philosophy — Vision → Mission → Values

Situational Analysis → Strategy Generation

Guidelines → Targets → Strategy Generation → Strategy Definition → Box score

Internal and external analysis

Projects → Execution

Procedure

Hoshin Kanri is also a one page tool to help leaders communicate the vision, strategy, and projects and will be used to manage the execution. As you can see, this is a very simple, but powerful tool that every manager should understand and continually practice, even for planning every person's life.

	TOP MANAGEMENT (Guidelines)				MANAGEMENT PLANNING (Strategies)				TACTICAL PLANNING – EXECUTION
GUIDELINE	DESCRIPTION	KPI's	Baseline	Objective	STRATEGIES	KPI's	Baseline	Objective	KEY ACTIVITIES / IMPROVEMENT PROJECTS
1. Increase Profitability									
2. Increase Sales									
3. Become a world-class company (reduce expenses)									
4. Make HR a competitive advantage									

In the LSSM – Fieldbook you can work through Hoshin Kanri examples.

2.5 KPI - KEY PERFORMANCE INDICATORS AND BOX SCORE

When the company has a Strategic Plan, then it is necessary to make it work through project implementation and continuous follow up of the results. This is when we have to define the key indicators (KPI's) for every level of the organization in order to understand the real functioning of the system. The KPI's translate what happens in the operation and reveal whether the strategies lead to a sustainable course.

KPI's

There are three level of indicators:

- **A. Value Added Level:** This are the floor indicators that normally are established every day and analyzed every hour, presented in daily score boards.

FLOOR INDICATORS

				DOWNTIME		
	HOUR	GOAL	REAL	MINUTES	TYPE	DEFECTS
1	8 to 9	10	10			
2	9 to 10	8	7	10	Break	
3	10 to 11	10	10			
4	11 to 12	10	5	20	Setup	
5	12 to 1	5	4	30	Lunch	
6	1 to 2	10	11			
7	2 to 3	10	2	30	Breakdown	3
8	3 to 4	10	12			
	TOTALS	73	61	90		3

- **B. Value Stream or Business Box Score:** These indicators are connected with daily indicators and are important to make good decisions at the business or plan level. This is called the Box Score, and these indicators are going to be analyzed every week.

By using the weekly Box Score, teams now have 52 opportunities (52 weeks of the year) to make better decisions and take corrective or preventive actions, if necessary, contrary to only 12 opportunities when it is done monthly.

The Box Score allows us to learn different perspectives of the business and keep focused on the team, instead of having separate indicators or functions.

KPI'S	BASE LINE	GOAL	WEEK 1	WEEK 2	WEEK 3	WEEK 4	WEEK 5
Net Promoter Score	55%	70%	51%	54%	49%	55%	57%
Days to launch new products	123	45	123	123	94	94	94
Market Share	12%	15%	11%	12%	12%	12%	13%
Facility Sigma Level	3.3	4.2	3.3	3.3	3.3	3.4	3.8
On-time deliveries	78%	99%	77%	76%	79%	70%	79%
OEE	53%	78%	51%	49%	55%	61%	68%
Delivery time (days)	12	8	12	12	12	12	10
Inventory turns	4	12	4	4	4	4	7
Cost of poor quality	125 K	12 K	29K	111K	121K	135 K	122 K
Certification progress	21%	78%	21%	21%	21%	25%	28%
Suggestions per person	0.2	1	0	0	0	0	0
Accidents	3	0	0	0	0	0	0
Demand	2500	7500	2450	2355	2143	3450	4597
Production Capacity	7500	10000	7500	7500	7500	7800	7800
Available capacity		25%	67%	69%	71%	56%	41%
Inventory Value	24 m	2450	$23,900,000	$24,100,000	$23,123,000	$22,913,400	$22,098,123
Revenue	3.5 m	7500	$3,304,500	$3,445,670	$3,120,670	$3,872,100	$3,850,215
Material Costs	2.45 m	67%	$2,511,420	$2,471,969	$2,122,056	$2,594,307	$2,541,142
Conversion Costs	1.2 m	2450	$1,234,980	$1,345,670	$1,234,700	$1,129,000	$1,150,570
Value Stream Profit	-0.15 m	7500	-$ 441,900	-$ 311,969	-$ 236,086	$148,793	$156,503
Value Stream ROS	0%	67%	-13.37%	-9.05%	-7.57%	3.84%	4.12%

Lean thinking practice using the Box Score is going to help us to always keep in mind what is important for the customers, employees, and the owners. It will also give us the opportunity to manage a system where we no longer measure people or departments, but the system as a whole.

- **C. Corporate level:** This set of indicators is needed when there is more than one business unit and is normally going to be analyzed every month using the Balance Scorecard:

BALANCE SCORECARD

TOP MANAGEMENT					MONTH 1–12						
OBJECTIVES	DESCRIPTION	INDICATORS	Baseline	Objective	1	2	3	4	5	6	7
1. Increase Profitability	Increase ROI from 7% to 12%	ROI Company	7%	12%	7%	7.1%	7.3%	8.2%	8.1%	9.4%	9.5%
2. Increase Sales	Increase domestic sales from 10% to 15% and international sales from 29% to 32%	Sales Domestic	10%	15%	2%	3.1%	2.1%	2.2%	4.5%	4.7%	5.6%
		Sales international	29%	32%	28%	28.2%	17.3%	27%	29.5%	32%	29%
3. Become a world-class company (reduce expenses)	Increase productivity of the operation from 10% to 15%, reducing defects and improving customer satisfaction NPS > 70 %, cost reduction of 11%	Productivity	25%	45%	22.3%	23%	21%	25%	24.3%	28%	31%
		Cost from Sales	15%	< 11%	15%	17%	14%	17%	14%	13%	12%
		NPS	40%	70%	45%	44%	49%	57%	66%	67%	64%
4. Make HR a competitive advantage	Achieve less than 1% annual turnover	Turnover Company	7%	1%	8%	9%	5%	3%	3%	4%	3%

It is important to notice that KPI's of all levels are connected to Corporate Level Indicators. They are deployed to the Box Score Level and the indicators connected to Process or Activity Level in order to align actions and results to the same system.

2.6 VALUE STREAM STRUCTURE AND MAPPING

Most companies are traditionally organized in a structure similar to the way in which family trees are done.

Functional organizations have the advantage of being very clear about the hierarchical differences in positions and levels, but the major disadvantage is that communication is poor and horizontal decision-making is lacking.

FUNCTIONAL ORGANIZATIONS
VERTICAL STRUCTURE

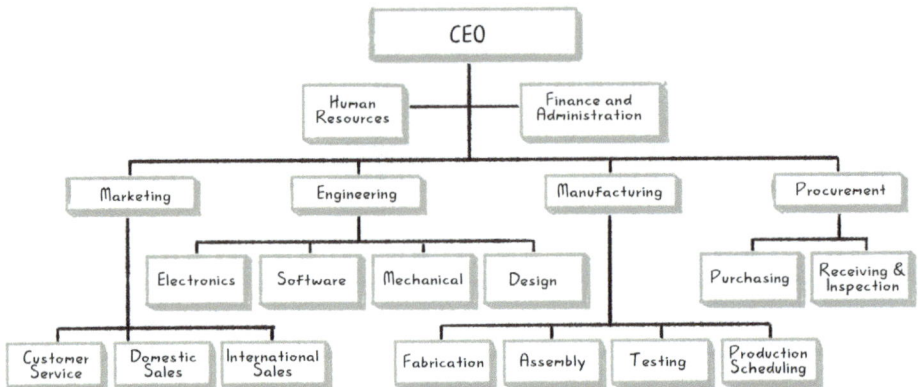

```
                                    CEO

                   Human                      Finance and
                   Resources                  Administration

      Marketing          Engineering            Manufacturing          Procurement

              Electronics  Software  Mechanical  Design        Purchasing  Receiving &
                                                                           Inspection

  Customer   Domestic  International      Fabrication  Assembly  Testing  Production
  Service    Sales     Sales                                              Scheduling
```

This type of structure worked relatively well when only few products or services were performed at high volume levels. Now that the market has changed to demanding a variety of products in small quantities quickly, it is almost impossible to use this same type of structure. Communication is a key element of a *Lean Six Sigma Management Company* in order to achieve agility and versatility. Unfortunately, the traditional functional structure does not allow an effective flow of information to the entire staff. While each department adds value, the company's bureaucracy increases the complexity of the work.

Value Streams are business units composed of some multidisciplinary teams of people directly responsible for creating value for the customer from the time the order is placed until the cash payment for the order is received. A Value Stream flowchart tracks the processes from beginning to end to meet the needs of customers for a range of services or products without a complex bureaucracy.

Each Value Stream is composed of a family of products that share processing by similar operations during the production process. Organizing a company by Value Streams is returning to the basics of when the company started by having a team of people from different areas completely focused on delivering customer value and taking responsibility for the whole process, analyzing information, and making decisions. What about your organization? Is it set up correctly? If not, are changes necessary?

VALUE STREAM STRUCTURE

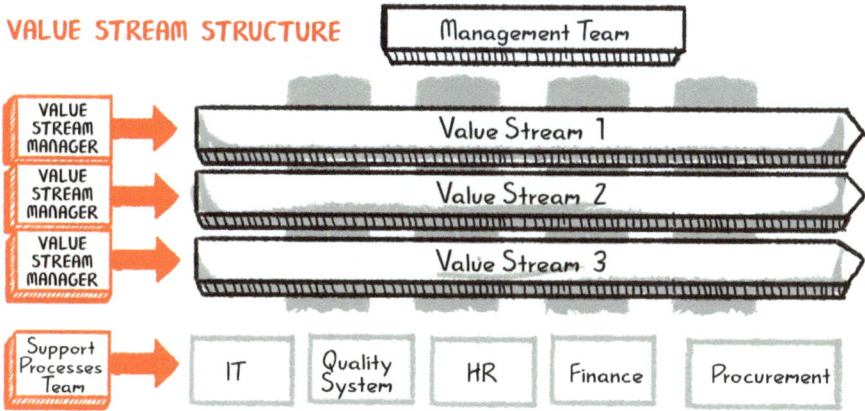

Management Team	

VALUE STREAM MANAGER	Value Stream 1
VALUE STREAM MANAGER	Value Stream 2
VALUE STREAM MANAGER	Value Stream 3

Support Processes Team	IT	Quality System	HR	Finance	Procurement

One of the biggest causes of failure when developing strategies and practicing Lean Six Sigma is the fact that many companies develop projects and implement tools in all places and at the same time, without establishing an accurate approach to the needs.

Value Stream Maps provide detailed knowledge of any process in a company; I.e. including service, manufacturing, and the entire supply chain. The Value Stream Map provides an understanding of the flow of a process and helps in the detection of non-value-added activities.

VALUE STREAM MAP

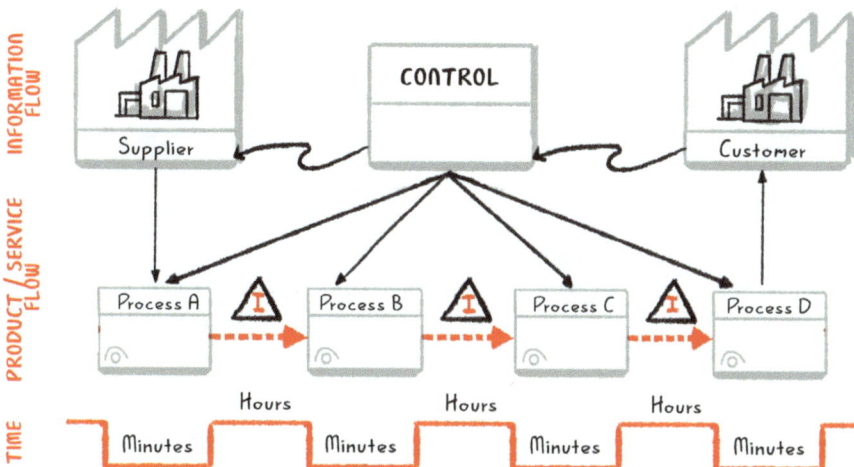

INFORMATION FLOW

PRODUCT / SERVICE FLOW

TIME

Supplier — CONTROL — Customer

Process A — Process B — Process C — Process D

Hours — Hours — Hours

Minutes — Minutes — Minutes — Minutes

The Value stream map is used as a strategic tool for establishing improvement plans and projects with specific approaches and objectives. Therefore, the strategy and project implementation have better chances to be successful when we are focusing on the main constraints.

Types of Maps

Current State Map
The current state map is a reference document to determine activities that do not add value in the process and document the current situation of the value chain.

Future State Map
The map of future state presents the best short-term solution of the operation, taking into account the improvements to be incorporated in the production system.

Value stream process
- Establishes the strategy to be developed in the process before executing changes
- Views the process in multiple levels
- Views the flow and sources of waste
- Provides a common language for process analysis
- Provides a model for creating flow and implementing Lean Six Sigma concepts and techniques
- Detects bottlenecks
- Detects areas of opportunity

Elements of a Value Stream Map
At the top of the map, you will find the flow of information moving from right to left connecting the customer requirements in terms of quantity and how often they order products or services. In the middle, you can see the steps of the process to produce a product or service connected with a push arrow and inventories between every step.

Finally, in the bottom is the value-added time required by every step and the non-value added represented by the inventory or in case of service, it will be a queue.

Develop a current Value Stream Map
1. Define the scope of the process by selecting any internal process that is generating the main problem of the company. Example (Order entry, emergency department in a hospital, manufacturing process, etc.
2. Define product or service family by grouping product or service with similar steps or equipment.
3. Develop the current value stream map to find the bottleneck in the system and recognize all forms of waste within the process.

4. Develop the future value stream map where you can establish the potential solution and expected results. This map represents your tactical plan to execute your strategy.

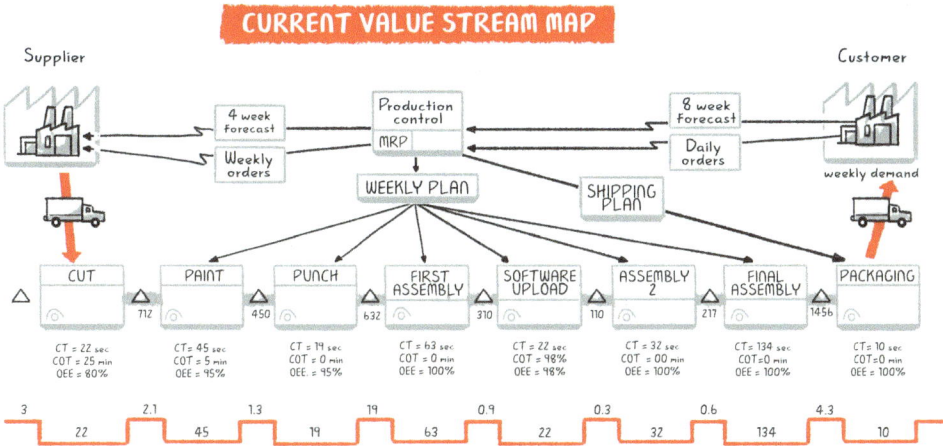

CURRENT VALUE STREAM MAP

Supplier   Customer

CUT	PAINT	PUNCH	FIRST ASSEMBLY	SOFTWARE UPLOAD	ASSEMBLY 2	FINAL ASSEMBLY	PACKAGING
CT = 22 sec	CT= 45 sec	CT = 19 sec	CT = 63 sec	CT = 22 sec	CT = 32 sec	CT= 134 sec	CT= 10 sec
COT = 25 min	COT = 5 min	COT = 0 min	COT = 0 min	COT = 98%	COT = 00 min	COT=0 min	COT=0 min
OEE = 80%	OEE = 95%	OEE = 95%	OEE = 100%	OEE = 98%	OEE = 100%	OEE = 100%	OEE = 100%

712 450 632 310 110 217 1456

3 2.1 1.3 19 0.9 0.3 0.6 4.3
22 45 19 63 22 32 134 10

Future Value Stream Map

The future value map presents the best possible solution and the most important projects to be developed in order to achieve the desired results of the strategic plan. It is important that top managers understand the value stream map so they can realize the level of the impact from all the projects and improvements to be made. It is recommended that every company, business unit, or plant develop a Current and Future Value Stream Map at least twice a year, along with a set of improvement events to be developed as part of the tactical plan.

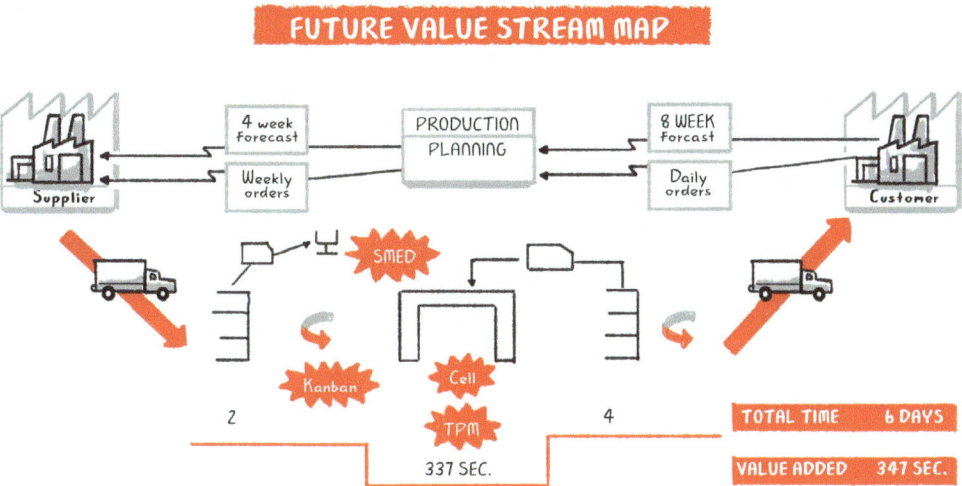

FUTURE VALUE STREAM MAP

2 4

337 SEC.

TOTAL TIME   6 DAYS

VALUE ADDED   347 SEC.

Results obtained

VSM IMPROVEMENTS	UNIT	CURRENT	FUTURE	UNIT IMPROVEMENT	% IMPROVEMENT
Total area used	SQ/Meters	1259	640	619	49%
Operators	Emloyees	10	5	5	50%
Walking distance	Meters	185	92	93	50%
Time door to door	Days	14.4	6	8.4	58%
Inventory - RM	Days	3	2	1	33%
Inventory - WIP	Days	7.1	0	7.1	100%
Inventory - FG	Days	4.3	4	0.3	7%
Inventory	Turnover/y	16.7	40	23.3	240%

We use the Future Value Stream Map to
- Understand the entire supply chain in a single document
- Establish the strategy to be developed before executing changes
- Visualize the process in multiple levels
- Provide a common language for process analysis
- Provide a model to create flow and implement Lean Six Sigma tools
- Define future goals and performance achievements

How to develop a Future Value Stream Map
1. Calculate the capacity of the process
2. Identify the best way to connect all steps of the process in a continuous flow
3. Draw the future value stream required to produce better results
4. Quantify possible results
5. Develop a future state plan

The most important point to understand is the amount of improvement in terms of delivery time, quality improvement, inventory reduction, and competitive advantage that the company is gaining among others. As the previous graph showed (Results obtained), amazing productivity improvement can be achieved by doing the Value Stream Map process carefully.

In the LSSM – Fieldbook, you can examine more examples of Value Stream Maps, one for services and one for a manufacturing process. You can also work through your own value stream map.

2.7 AGILE PROJECT MANAGEMENT WITH SCRUM

The most important part of strategic management is execution; therefore, Project Management helps companies to develop their strategies through successful project deployment and implementation.

The Hoshin Kanri and the Value Stream Map have as deliverables a set of important projects to be developed. This is when company leaders have to decide what type of Project Management methodology will be adopted to ensure a correct project implementation and therefore achieve the expected results.

No more than 20% of companies make a Strategic Plan. Of those who do, only 8% are successful in implementing the strategy. The main cause of failure is the inadequate management of their projects. Very few companies are prepared with project management skills even though all companies develop projects. Maybe that is why no more than 10% develop projects on time and with good results.

Agile Project Management is a very powerful way to manage complex projects in an environment with high uncertainty. In 1986, Professors Hirotaka Takeuchi and Ikujiro Nonaka published the article, "The New Product Development Game," published by Harvard Business Review.

They studied more productive and innovative teams in companies globally, such as Honda, Fuji-Xerox, 3 M, etc. They argued that the old way of developing products (waterfall) has origin faults. The best companies followed a faster and more flexible linked development process.

Teams were inter-functional and flexible. Management was not giving orders, executives were service leaders and facilitators, dedicated in removing obstacles. They compared the work with a rugby game.

SCRUM is a process like rugby, where the whole team works collaboratively to win. After this article was published, Ken Schwaber and Jeff Sutherland developed SCRUM as a framework to develop successful projects. In 2001, a group of 17 experts including Ken Schwaber and Jeff Sutherland, created what is called the agile manifesto.

Benefits of using SCRUM
- Align individual and corporate goals
- Create a culture based on performance
- Support the creation of value for shareholders
- Achieve stable and consistent levels of communication at all levels

SCRUM is a framework, in which people can solve complex problems, productively and creatively, generating products of the highest possible value.

SCRUM elements
- Roles of the participants: Product Owner, Team Members, SCRUM Master
- Scrum Events: Sprint Planning, Daily SCRUM, Sprint review, Sprint retrospective
- Artifacts: Product Backlog, Sprint Backlog, Burndown chart

Product Owner Responsibilities
- Improve the speed of project development
- Align individual and corporate goals
- Create a culture based on performance
- Support the creation of value for shareholders
- Achieve stable and consistent levels of communication at all levels

Team Member responsibilities
- Self-organized teams of 5 - 10 multi-functional members: QA, Designers, Engineers, etc.
- Teams may vary between Sprints
- Develop project activities and tasks

SCRUM Master responsibilities
- Ensures that SCRUM is understood and practiced correctly
- Organizes and motivates team members
- Prepares meetings and monitors the development of projects
- Helps in obstacle removal

SCRUM is an agile and effective project management system because it takes time for every project to:

- **Define Project Vision** to establish goals and align every project to the strategies already established in the Hoshin Kanri
- **Map the Project** to develop a high-level plan to describe all of the characteristics the project should have in order to accomplish the vision
- **Develop a Release Plan** to have the team focused and have a complete understanding of all the components of the project in a product backlog
- **Develop a Sprint Plan** where the rhythm of the project is established to deliver functional deliverables or minimal viable products to work smart and learn continuously. Every sprint or project deliverable is carefully designed
- **Multi-Functional and Self-Guided Teams** develop minimal viable deliverables. Project tasks are self-assigned in order to manage the rhythm of the project, assuring on time delivery and high-quality deliverables
- **Meetings** are conducted every day, so all team members demonstrate their commitment and express their concerns

- **Present the deliverables** at the end of every sprint, so the team demonstrates a functional product every one to four weeks, analyzing in retrospect what worked well and what the downsides were to develop improvement ideas for the next sprints

In the next figure you can see how scrum is developed in order to deliver great results in record time to ensure a successful strategy execution.

PREPARATION   **SPRINT EVENT**   **DELIVERABLES**

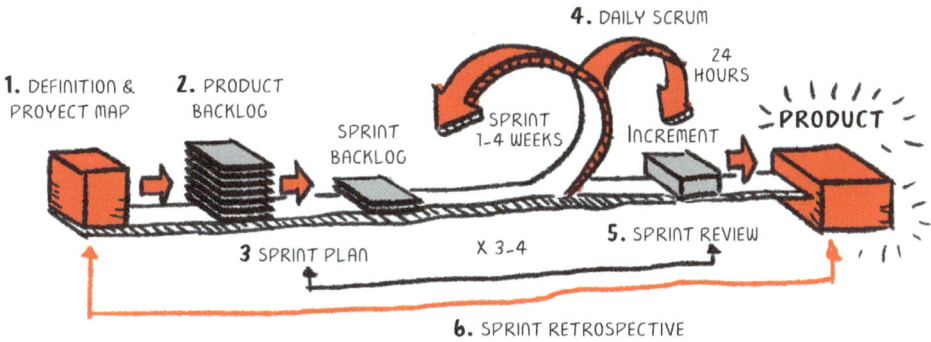

4. DAILY SCRUM

24 HOURS

1. DEFINITION & PROYECT MAP   **2.** PRODUCT BACKLOG   SPRINT BACKLOG   SPRINT 1-4 WEEKS   INCREMENT   PRODUCT

3 SPRINT PLAN   X 3-4   **5.** SPRINT REVIEW

6. SPRINT RETROSPECTIVE

In the LSSM – Fieldbook, you can work through a SCRUM example and have the opportunity to practice to develop your own SCRUM for any situation or project.

2.8 STANDARD WORK FOR LEADERS

First of all, let us explain Standard Work. Standard Work is a defined routine for a task being done on a regular basis. Imagine an airline flight where everyone from pilot to all flight attendants and support personnel has clear standard tasks.

If we implement Lean Six Sigma, it it's important that we will have standard work instructions in all areas, even for management and team leaders.

WHAT IS LEADER STANDARD WORK?

A set of daily/weekly actions tools and behaviors that leaders apply to build and sustain a continuous improvement culture

Most organizations that implement a Lean Six Sigma philosophy usually lack a key ingredient to maintain a Lean Management System. A lean culture is the result of a good and living management system. This culture is built through a set of activities and habits that start by eliminating waste, which will gradually become the way we behave and act, and finally, it will become the way we are.

A healthy management system derives from a healthy Value Stream. Leaders Standard Work is the engine of the management system and the most influential tool in the transformation to a Lean culture. It is therefore the reason that we mention standard work for leaders in this strategy chapter. It helps leaders move from a focus on results to a twofold focus on the processes and results. It generates the necessary behaviors to transform the culture, creating a new environment of collaborative work and high satisfaction. It helps new managers become high-performance leaders, eliminates improvisation of team leaders and managers and challenges leaders to become teachers, coaches, and facilitators in solving problems.

Why Leader Standard Work?

The management system will be clearly documented. It will document every activity that leaders should perform during their day, focusing on only value-added activities. It will define the expected behavior for leaders to show everyone what the really important activities to focus on are. Leader Standard Work is going to help you have a structured and documented system that can be learned and taught by new leaders. This is a way to configure the workplace. It is dependent on the process, not on people. It is a systematic approach to identifying opportunities, and finally, it is a list of activities that must be done to maintain the work system: audits, meetings, project reviews, etc. When good operators become supervisors or team leaders, they do not always have the necessary skills and/or knowledge. They stop doing activities where they are experts and become bureaucratic managers. Usually, their roles are not described.

Standard Work for Leaders: In a food processing company, we supported a Lean Six Sigma implementation, we learned that all the leaders had different priorities, goals, focuses, and were rarely on the floor due to so many non-value added administrative activities. In multiple workshops, we defined the daily, weekly and monthly Standard Work. Now, all activities were aligned to the vision, strategy, Hoshin Kanri, and the priorities. The leaders became more effective, and employees on the floor were happy to see the managers and be helped. Results improved quickly.

Team leaders are not always supervised, and generally, they work in a reactive scenario. Their talent and experience are wasted, resulting in them overseeing rather than guiding. They do not always teach what they know because of lack of time or because they think that is not their responsibility.

In 1911, Frederick Taylor, developed the scientific management of work, which would lead to Standardized Work.

In the following example, you can see how documenting the work schedule of every leader can give more focus to management activities and reserve time for important activities, such as training, time dedicated to projects, learning, coaching etc.

Please see the LSSM - Fieldbook for tips and formats for implementing Standard Work for leaders.

LEADER STANDARD WORK

TIME	TASK
8:00	Meeting (on-the floor)
8:15	Gemba Walk
8:30	Review Alicia and Jorge's LSW
8:45	Emails / Voice Mail
9:00	Prepare for a meeting
9:15	Meeting
9:30	Meeting
9:45	Production Board / Open items
10:00	Review first production run performance
10:15	
10:30	Task Follow-up
10:45	
11:00	Project time
11:15	Project time
11:30	Project time
11:45	Project time
12:30	Review 2nd production run performance
12:45	
1:00	Results presentation meeting and task follow-up
1:15	Time for pending tasks
1:30	Time for pending tasks
1:45	
2:00	
2:15	
2:30	Review 3rd production run performance
2:45	
3:00	
3:15	Costing simulations
3:30	
3:45	
4:00	
4:15	Review on-time delivery performance

DAY	TIME	TASK
MON	9:00	Production and shipping schedule
TUE	11:00	Training Session
WED	9:00	Meeting
THU		
FRI		

MONTHLY		
1st Monday	9:00	Montly production report
2nd Tuesday	9:00	Project Review
3rd Tuesday	9:00	Cross-training review

SHEET EXAMPLE

2.9 KATA

Most companies are led and run by hardworking people, who want their teams and organization to succeed. Sometimes, there is a feeling of frustration because of the difference between the desired results and what really happens. The problem is not the employees; it's usually the management system in place.

A management system is the systematic search of the desired situations through the use of human capabilities and competences in a coordinated way. It is true that we cannot predict the future, but we can adjust continually to the continuous dynamic of change and customer requirements.

KATA represents the way Toyota manages continuous improvement and adaptability to changing situations. Kata are routine practices that help us adopt new ways of acting and thinking. It is a pattern of scientific thinking that is combined with practical routines that help us adopt new ways of thinking and acting.

KATA is repeating a four-step routine by which an organization improves and adapts. It makes continuous improvement through the scientific problem-solving method of Plan, Do, Check, and Act.

The four steps are:

Practicing Kata is going to help us achieve the goal we seek in a process, without generating disconnected ideas, but with a focused model of improvements based on well-founded hypotheses, experiments, and frequent follow-ups.

We develop structured routines for exercising teamwork and learning. It is a way to transfer skills, develop skills, and share ways of thinking within a team or organization.

Lean Six Sigma Management System only works if we provide learning and improving experiences every day, not just when we practice Kaizen events. The responsibility of the manager is not to develop solutions, but to develop the skills of his employees.

Elements for conducting KATA's

I. In order to develop KATA, we are going to use a whiteboard, called a Kata-Board. The Kata-Board is located on the floor or in the office where the work and results will be improved.
II. A Question card is used to read the questions when a KATA is conducted. It generally contains five questions to be asked by the leader of the area where the KATA is conducted.
III. The Obstacle list is where we write all the obstacles that prevent reaching the objective condition or at least the most important obstacles.
IV. An Improvement cycle record is used by the operator to document the experiments, the results, and what was learned.

Leaders at all levels conduct KATA's with their partners who work in the service and manufacturing processes. KATA is conducted whenever we seek to achieve an objective condition that we have not achieved in terms of quality, cost, delivery, safety, morale, etc.

KATA is a simple process that takes from 10 to 15 minutes every time it's conducted, but doing it continually solves big problems, in a small time frame.

How Katas are conducted?

1. Leaders decide the place and process
2. A specific time is scheduled each time a Kata is conducted
3. The Leader of the process asks the questions listed in the card
4. The process owner responds to the questions
5. Experiments are conducted by the process team
6. New KATA's will be conducted by the leaders to find the results of the experiments and what was learned

You will find more about how to set up KATA, examples, implementation and follow through in the LSSM - Fieldbook

2.10 GEMBA - WALK

The problems are visible and improvement ideas will come from going to the Gemba. This means we are going to where things happen and where people need support. The Gemba walk is an activity that takes management to the front lines to look for waste and opportunities to practice a Kaizen event or make practical shop floor improvements.

*"When you are out observing on the Gemba, do something to help them" If you do, people will come to expect that you can help them and will look forward to seeing you again on the Gemba". **Taiichi Ohno***

Fujio Cho, Former Toyota CEO established these guidelines for Gemba Walks:
- Go and see
- Spend time on the line
- Ask why?
- "Use the why, literally everyday"
- Show respect

Observe and learn
- Adopt a student's mindset during a Gemba Walk
- Keep an open mind and ask many open-ended questions
- Learn, don't judge to give unjustified advice

Lean Six Sigma has become a worldwide improvement philosophy that uses some standardized tools (VSM, Kanban, Cells, SMED, 5 S's, Hoshin Kanri, etc.). Applying the tools appropriate to the situation, has provided good results, but these results are only sustained for a certain period of time (1 - 2 years).

Improvement programs need strong leaders in order to maintain the system and constantly improve the results. If this is not the case, the improvement programs are terminated or abandoned, because there are no leaders to maintain them. See picture below:

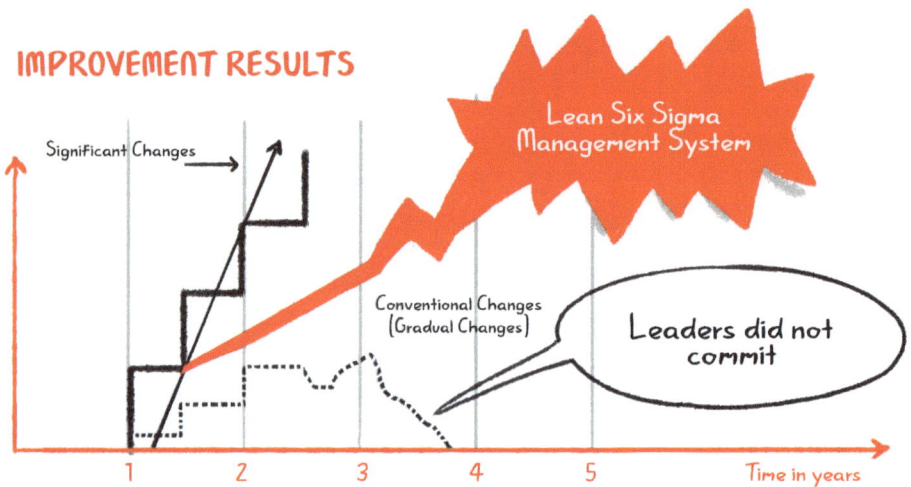

World-class business leaders spend at least 80% of their time planning, training, and executing high-level strategies. But what do they do the rest of their time? If you spend less than 25% of the time at the place where things happen (Gemba), then you need to adjust your priorities. You will need to adjust your time schedule in order to support the Lean Six Sigma strategy.

What Gemba is not?
- Walking around without a purpose
- An opportunity to find fault with others
- A time for problem solving and making changes
- View the workplace using a camera while sitting at a desk
- The desk of a manager is not Gemba

The purpose of Gemba walks is to focus, learn, and observe the processes, not to evaluate personal performance of employees.

Why walk the process?
- To understand how value is really created in the organization
- To see and reconcile the value creation process (horizontal) with the leadership direction (vertical)
- Build relationships and trust between leaders and staff
- Show leadership commitment to Lean Six Sigma initiatives
- Promote accountability within the organization

Gemba walks are made by:
- Presidents and Vice-Presidents
- General managers
- Functional managers
- Value Chain managers
- Area Leaders
- Team Leaders

"There was a perception that he was going to upset people. Over time, they have understood that he just wanted to see the process as a customer. I can do my job better if I have firsthand information on "the good, the bad and the ugly." **Bob Nardelli - Home Depot CEO**

2.11 TALENT MANAGEMENT

Toyota not only produces vehicles, but is a best-in-class example for developing great talent, and although many have tried to copy their model to improve performance, most have failed because they do not devote enough time to developing people. Unfortunately, many companies spend little time on training and developing employees because of the daily to do list and emergencies. The little training provided to employees does not support achieving its objectives, and therefore, the results are ineffective. This becomes a vicious cycle that never seems to end, and usually, the best employees leave the company because of little or no support.

In recent decades, developing the human potential remains the biggest challenge of any organization. We always say that the human resource is the most important resource in the company, but most of the time, we experience the opposite. Companies spend far more time on investment projects, budgets, problem solving and so on, and the human resource doesn't have much time left. We find companies with advanced implementation of quality systems, but we have seen that the cause of many of the problems of quality, productivity, and especially communication occur because not enough time was dedicated to training or on-boarding new employees.

What is a Talent Development System?

When the United States faced the possibility of entering the Second World War, the government started to plan how to transmit skills and knowledge to women and older people when the male workforce would be sent to fight in the war. The U.S. Government developed the TWI (Training Within Industry) program to train unqualified staff to replace workers who went to war. A team of trainers and professionals in the field developed a method to document the critical knowledge of any company, preparing trainers to be able to teach essential skills to perform their jobs in an active and effective way (Skill Leadership Skill Training and Skill Enhancement).

The purpose of the process was to develop the knowledge and commitment of people to be able to do their job properly and provide customers with quality products and/or services at the target cost and in the shortest time possible.

It is a methodology to create a culture of learning and training of employees, so that each person can reach their full potential. As previously stated, people are the most important element and resource, because even if everything else changes, your employees can make everything work if they are prepared.

Talent Development – in-house university: An automotive parts supplier company had little to no training or talent development in the company. Costs needed to be kept low and employees had to be rapidly productive. Employees began working shortly after they started at the new company on day one. It's not possible to implement a *Lean Six Sigma Management System* in this type of environment. The best-in-class talent development program we have seen was a company that implemented a strong, but simple in-house university where 100% of employees (including the whole management team) had to go through required training and exams year after year. After three to six months, a performance review evaluated their achievements, necessary adjustments, and actions to be taken. The complete training and development plan (including the manager's) was displayed to all employees on a large white board on the hallway of the company. Every month, the implemented actions and achievements would change the individual actions to green, yellow or red. This is an example of how to make talent development a key focus.

Basically, there are three phases for talent development:

1. Attracting talent (in-house or outside)

A process needs to be in place in order to develop the right talent (in-or outside the company):

- *Recruitment* - need to make sure we interview the right employees
- *Selection* - make sure you have hired the right person, skills, experience, values, inspiration, drive, personal objectives
- *On-boarding* - a good plan will insure an effective and complete training program to get the person up to speed ASAP

2. Developing talent
Once the employee has been on-boarded, the process continues:

- Prepare the organization,
- Identify critical knowledge
- Transfer knowledge
- Promoting and disseminating

3. Mature & Inspire
On a continuous basis, make sure the employee prospers, matures, and stays inspired:

- Performance assessment
- Compensation
- Training

2.12 KEY POINTS

1. Good Strategic Planning is the key to the success of any project. Invest enough time in order to define what you want to achieve.

2. Start with a Lean Company Assessment, this will provide you the areas on which to focus.

3. Prepare a strong Change Management Process.

4. A Business Model is a map of how the business is going to create and deliver value to their customers and how it is intended to generate revenue and profits.

5. Use the Strategy Wheel, the purpose in the middle of the wheel is your Vision – Mission - Purpose of your company. It's all about aligning your functions and plans to the center.

6. Hoshin Kanri helps as a framework based on the cooperation of the whole company to deploy the long-term strategic objectives and the short-term management plan.

7. Define meaningful KPI's and use the Box Score to review results per day, week, month, quarter, and year.

8. Value Stream Structure and Mapping provides detailed knowledge and understanding of any process in a company; i.e., service, manufacturing, and the entire supply chain. The Value Stream Map provides an understanding of the flow of a process and helps in the detection of non-value-added activities.

9. Agile Project Management will be required and SCRUM is a great framework, in which people can solve complex problems, productively and creatively generating products or projects of the highest possible value.

10. Don't forget the Talent Management – without a strong and dedicated team we will not achieve the goals.

11. GEMBA Walks help the whole team see the process as a customer does and improves it day by day.

Please add your additional Key Points:

_____
_____
_____
_____
_____

CHAPTER 3

3. TACTICAL TOOLS

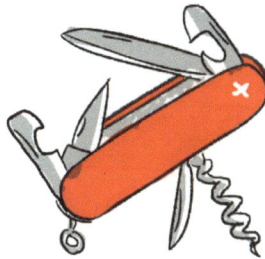

3.1 THE LEAN SIX SIGMA TACTICAL TOOL BOX

After reviewing the Strategic Tools, we will now concentrate on the Tactical Tools. During our years of supporting companies to achieve excellence, we have learned to use the most effective, obvious, and simple Lean Six Sigma tools. During your company's transformation, you and your team will use the *Lean Six Sigma Management* tools as required, depending on your plans, actual situation and the results of the assessments done.

Let's review the data and trends again.

Analysis of Performance

In our maturity model, a collaborative analysis should take place to identify opportunities and define specific actions in accordance with the behavior or the trends of the key performance indicators.

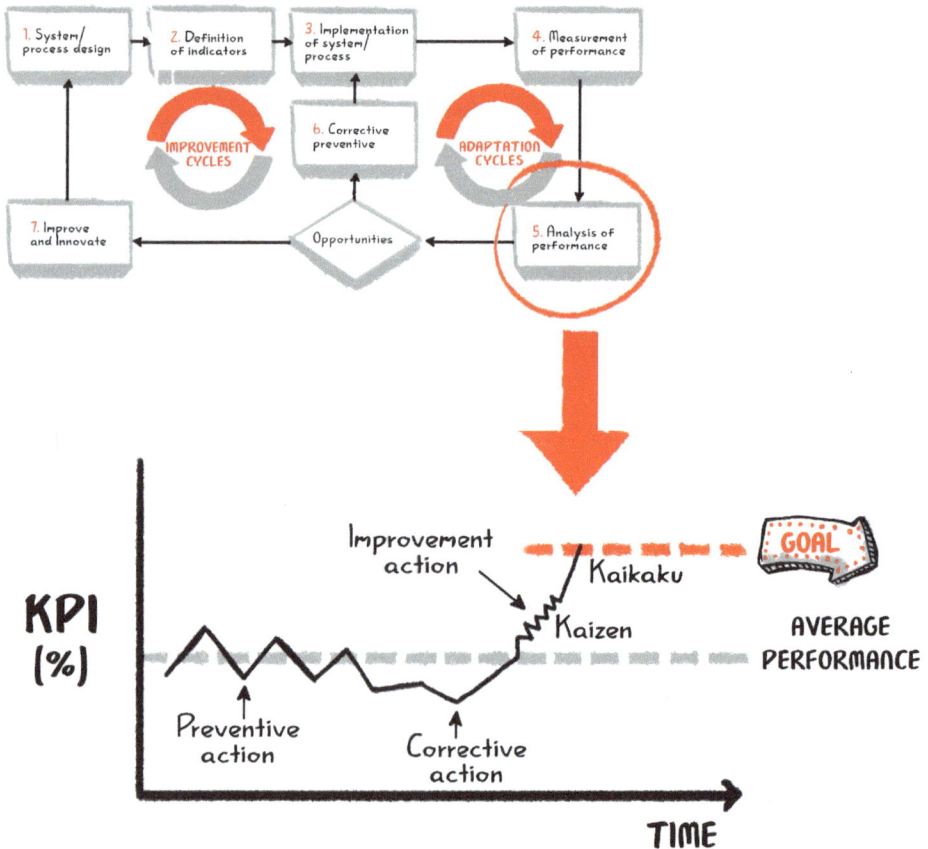

Once the team has reviewed and analyzed the indicators in the Balance Scorecard, Box Score, or Floor Board and understands the reasons for the results, then we can decide what type of cycle we are going to follow and what type of tool(s) we may choose out of the toolbox.

Which cycle to use? Adaptation or Improvement Cycles?

Adaptation Cycle

Let's look at the adaptation cycle first. In these cycles, we develop corrective and preventive actions in order to stabilize and control processes using the Lean Six Sigma toolbox.

This type of Improvement Cycle is normally a quick event called a Kaizen Blitz (explained later in detail), which normally takes between half of a day to two days. An interdisciplinary and multiskilled team will first look into the key indicators, identify the problem, and choose the appropriate tool(s) from the toolbox in order to fix the current problem and prevent future reoccurrence. This is a quick Improvement Cycle and is normally done by the value stream team.

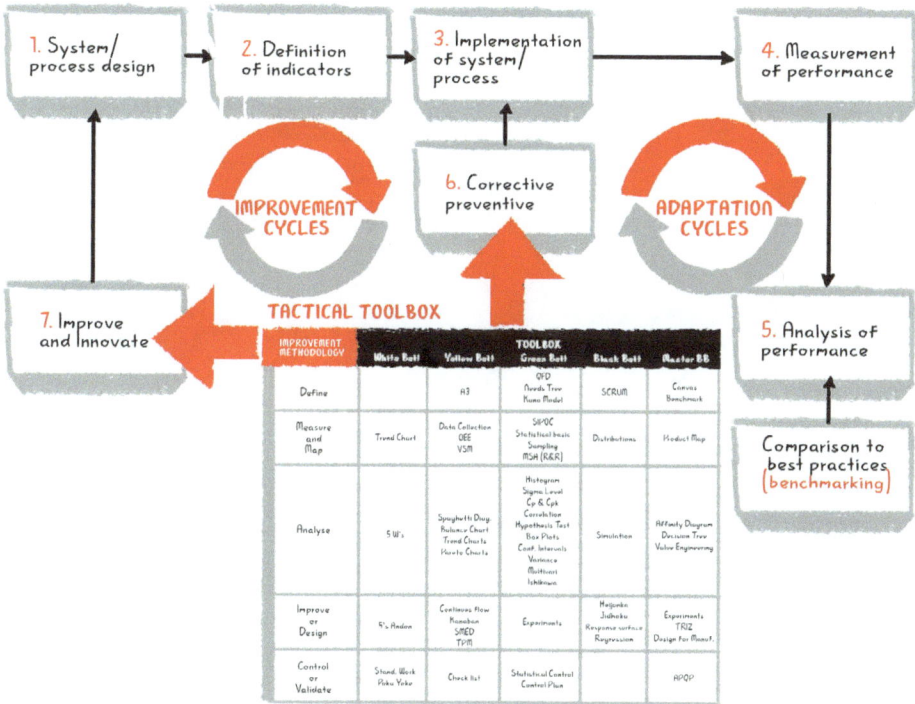

IMPROVEMENT METHODOLOGY	TOOLBOX				
	White Belt	Yellow Belt	Green Belt	Black Belt	Master BB
Define		A3	QFD Needs Tree Kano Model	SCRUM	Canvas Benchmark
Measure and Map	Trend Chart	Data Collection OEE VSM	SIPOC Statistical basis Sampling MSA (R&R)	Distributions	Product Map
Analyse	5 W's	Spaghetti Diag. Pareto Chart Trend Charts Pareto Charts	Histogram Sigma Level Cp & Cpk Correlation Hypothesis Test Box Plots Conf. Intervals Variance Multivari Ishikawa	Simulation	Affinity Diagram Decision Tree Value Engineering
Improve or Design	5's Andon	Continous Flow Kanban SMED TPM	Experiments	Heijunka Jidhoka Response surface Regression	Experiments TRIZ Design for Manuf.
Control or Validate	Stand. Work Poka Yoke	Check list	Statistical Control Control Plan		APQP

For details see next page

Improvement Cycle

Improvement (Kaizen): The team will choose this option when the goal has not been achieved and changes are required to reach the goals or solve complex problems. Here, the tools needed to improve performance use the DMAIC Methodology and Lean Six Sigma tools from the toolbox. The detailed Kaizen description will follow in the next few pages.

Innovation (Kaikaku): The team will choose this option when a discontinuous improvement, radical change, or innovation is required to make the vision and strategy occur. In this case, we suggest using the Design for Six Sigma Methodology: DMADV with innovation tools described in the following toolbox. The detailed Kaikaku description will follow in the next few pages.

The toolbox below includes all tools you and your team will learn to use in the different Lean Six Sigma Training Levels. We will review some of them later in this chapter.

TACTICAL TOOLBOX

IMPROVEMENT METHODOLOGY	TOOLBOX				
	White Belt	Yellow Belt	Green Belt	Black Belt	Master BB
Define		A3	QFD Needs Tree Kano Model	SCRUM	Canvas Benchmark
Measure and Map	Trend Chart	Data Collection OEE VSM	SIPOC Statistical basic Sampling MSA (R&R)	Distributions	Product Map
Analyse	5 W's	Spaghetti Diag. Balance Chart Trend Charts Pareto Charts	Histogram Sigma Level Cp & Cpk Correlation Hypothesis Test Box Plots Conf. Intervals Variance Multivari Ishikawa	Simulation	Affinity Diagram Decision Tree Value Engineering
Improve or Design	5's Andon	Continues Flow Kanaban SMED TPM	Experiments	Heijunka Jidhoka Response surface Regression	Experiments TRIZ Design for Manuf.
Control or Validate	Stand. Work Poka Yoke	Check list	Statistical Control Control Plan		APQP

In order to understand and master the tools, it is important to dedicate time and resources to make the cycles run smoothly to be able to take the company to the next development level faster than any other competitor.

The methodology and tools have shown that they can be applied in any type of industry and in any process or department within a company, not just for quality assurance or production systems.

As a leader it's important to be aware that this toolbox exists and that your team members from any level and department can learn and apply those tools continuously.

This toolbox was developed in a very flexible manner, so that other tools you learn or consider important could be integrated by you and your team as needed.

3.2 KAIZEN FOR IMPROVEMENT AND KAIKAKU FOR INNOVATION CYCLES

Kaizen and Kaikaku are both concepts from the Japanese production philosophy. Both have their origin from the Toyota Production System. Kaikaku means an Innovation change, whereas Kaizen means continuous minor changes (improvements).

Let's start with the Kaizen Process, the more well-known process. It has its origin in the Buddhist school of India, practiced in China, Korea, and Japan, where it seeks the improvement of a person.

Kaizen for improvement & problem solving

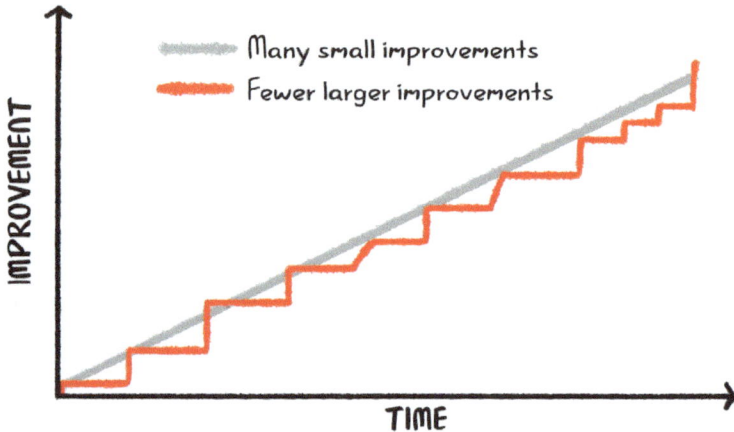

It is a continuous improvement process in order to sustainably improve a company process. Kaizen means continuous improvement, applied in gradual and orderly form. It involves all the employees in the organization. This is a great tool to improve a process without making large capital investments, actually with little money most of the time.

Kaizen events are extremely effective in rapidly improving a process by implementing Lean tools. Depending on the impact on the process and the difficulty of the process, it usually takes one to five days to carry it out. A Kaizen event is mainly an event with a specific start and finish, a dedicated team, with a clear objective to improve a poor performance situation or fix a recurring problem.

During the Kaizen event, we recommend using the **DMAIC methodology**:

- **Define:** Problem or situation to improve
- **Measure:** Get data and understand the process
- **Analyze:** Identify root cause and main constraints
- **Improve:** Develop activities to solve the problem or make an improvement
- **Control:** Develop countermeasures to maintain the result

Some examples of types of Kaizen events:

- Problem Solving (Kaizen Blitz) Time = 0.5 - 2 days mainly for problem solving
- Improvement Kaizen (2 -5 days)

Practicing Kaizen events will empower employees, enrich the work experience, bring out the best in each employee, and drive continuous improvement.

Benefits of Kaizen Events
- Promotes the personal growth of employees and the company
- Improves quality, safety, cost structures, delivery, environment, performance, and customer service/satisfaction
- Provides employee guidance and serves as a barometer for leadership
- Reduce customer response times
- Better distribution of space and area
- Better performance of equipment
- Better communication
- Greater capacity for attention to customers
- Better working conditions in safety and ergonomics
- Breaks paradigms

Types of Kaizen Events
- Housekeeping with 5 S's
- Visual control
- Total Productive Maintenance
- Cellular Manufacturing
- Quick product changes (SMED)
- Error-prone Poka Yoke
- Six Sigma
- Problem solving
- Prevention with FMEA
- Kanban
- Heijunka
- Continuous flow
- Reduce downtime or waste
- Improve safety
- Material supply and Kanban

Kaizen Event Leader

Each Kaizen event should be led by a facilitator. This must be a skilled team member that understands both the tools and the methodology.

The facilitator is an indispensable channel for connecting the results of the Kaizen event with the business goals raised by senior management (remember Hoshin Kanri). Experience has shown that the facilitators of successful teams have the following characteristics:

- Has skills as a coach and staff manager
- Recognized, trusted, and respected by members of the group
- Is not responsible for the Kaizen event or its outcome
- Works as a support for team members
- Does not necessarily belong to the area or department that carries out the Kaizen event, but is an expert in the methodology and tools while the team members are the experts in the process to improve
- Plays an essential role to keep the team's focus on the theme of the event as a source of information, as well as support for the enthusiasm of team members

Kaikaku for Innovation

Kaikaku stands for Innovation change in the system. Kaikaku is most often initiated by management, since the change and the result will have a significant business impact. Kaikaku is about introducing a new strategy, a new approach, new production techniques, or new equipment. Kaikaku can be initiated by external factors or when management sees that Kaizen is no longer providing better results.

We can find different types of Kaikaku projects depending on the degree of innovation:

- **Degree of low innovation:** implementation of methodologies already known in the market but not known in the company, which implies low costs with high impact on profits, or the development of new technologies within the company that are already known in the business world.

- **Degree of high innovation:** the development of a new technology within the company that is unknown in the market and that is introduced for the first time in the company, as well the introduction of new solutions with innovative methodologies that are also new to the company.

With Kaikaku, we will usually run several projects in parallel because the big change impact involves the whole organization, and results will not be seen immediately.

This is in Contrast with a Kaizen event where we usually run one project and will observe an immediate improvement.

At all times, we must have a series of previously agreed indicators that help to discern the progress of the project and the improvements implemented.

Keeping a storyboard of the Kaizen and Kaikaku events will help to remind us of the strengths and weaknesses of the projects already carried out and how to improve future events.

Kaikaku - DMADV Methodology
- **Define:** Problem or situation to improve
- **Map/Measure:** Get data and understand the process
- **Analyze:** Identify root cause and main constraints
- **Design:** Design or redesign product/service or components
- **Validate:** Validate if the design complies with the specifications

Some examples of types of Kaikaku Events

Time 1 – 5 weeks

Practicing Kaikaku events will empower teams, enrich the work experience, bring out the best from each employee, and drive continuous improvement.

Types of Kaikaku Events
- Design new products
- Design new services
- Design new plants
- Re-design current products
- Compare all critical parts for tear down analysis from other competitors
- Design for manufacturing products and parts
- Test products in the market
- Develop new concepts for new business models
- Re-design a complete process from beginning to end

Final thoughts about Innovation within *Lean Six Sigma Management*

Sometimes it appears that an innovation culture does not fit with a Lean Six Sigma culture. The system for boosting lean and quality culture may seem to run counter to disruptive change. It may appear crazy to tell people they should be focused on becoming more efficient while at the same time you want them to explore untapped growth potential.

What Innovation means: Change, alteration, revolution, upheaval, transformation, breakthrough, new measures, new methods, modernization, creativity, ingenuity, inspiration, etc. Innovation today is also Industry 4.0/

Industrial Internet of Things (IIoT), Smart Factory, disruptive innovation, and so on. The key question is: Can we do innovation while becoming Lean and strengthening the existing processes?

Our answer is: Absolutely! It has more to do with sufficient resources, project focus, and priorities, and also depends on the form of innovation we want to trigger.

Many forms of Innovation Cycles

- **Efficiency Innovation:** Efficiency innovation delivers ways to improve efficiency and speed of effectiveness. It can include internal systems and processes or ways to expedite the customer/client experience
- **Process Innovation:** Process Innovation encompasses the implementation of a new or significantly improved production or delivery method
- **Product Innovation:** Product Innovation is the introduction of a good or service that is new or substantially improved, which may include improvements in functional characteristics, technical abilities, ease, or any other dimension
- **Service Innovation:** Service Innovation, compared to goods or product innovation or process innovation, delivers ways to improve the delivery of a service and is both interactive and information intensive
- **System Innovation:** This form of Innovation includes introducing a new infrastructure or system, which could produce new sectors, and include major change across several areas of the business
- **Technological Innovation:** This may include coming up with new technologies to solve some problem or new uses for existing technologies. Solutions may be high tech or low tech
- **Financial Innovation:** This form of innovation focuses on ways to increase sales, reduce costs, improve tracking of expenses, reduce accounts receivables, improve tax/audit compliance, as well as other ways of managing finances to enhance profitability
- **Incremental Innovation:** This could be when one adds something extra to a product or service that the competition doesn't have or isn't doing or when one makes something last longer, be more convenient or faster
- **Marketing Innovation:** This involves development of new marketing methods with improvement in product design or packaging, product promotion, communication, advertising, pricing or distribution

A true *Lean Six Sigma Management* transformation will include innovation processes. Innovation is a substantial part and process of any company; no innovation equals no progress. On the other hand, *Lean Six Sigma Management* assures the perfect layout and setting of processes being lean with the right employees, product quality and service, customer driven, and the best return on investment.

Please see the LSSM - Fieldbook on how to plan a Kaizen or Kaikaku Event.

3.3 BASIC TOOLS: HOUSEKEEPING 5 S's, ANDON, STANDARDIZED WORK, POKA YOKE

Housekeeping – 5 S's

Habits are the most important element in the agile thinking culture. In order to start any type of improvement, it is very important to work in a safe and clean environment.

Ford Motor Company developed a program called CANDO, which stands for Cleaning, Arranging, Neatness, Discipline and Ongoing. After World War II, some Japanese managers who visited the Michigan plants adopted the program (Hiroyuki Hirano).

The application of the 5 S's (Housekeeping) was developed by Hiroyuki Hirano and represents one of the elements that frame the initiation of any tool or system of improvement. That is why it is said that a good improvement event is one that starts with the 5 S's.

Lean tools are a breakthrough in the implementation of process improvements that create value in a business. But, one of the elements of great importance in this involves the culture and habits that have been developed over time. That is why when we speak of order and cleanliness, we consider not only the application of a basic tool, but also the development of good habits of order and cleanliness that form the basis for the development and application of many other tools that will come later on.

BEFORE 5 S's

AFTER 5 S's

Sort	Straighten	Shine	Standardize	Sustain
SORT: Remove all items that are not needed from the work areas.	**STRAIGHTEN:** Organize necessary work items by establishing a specific place for each item.	**SHINE:** Very simple, clean the workspace!	**STANDARDIZE:** Ensure that the procedures and activities are implemented consistently.	**SUSTAIN:** Make a habit out of 5's activities (previous 4 steps) to ensure that work areas are more productive.

This discipline is known as 5 S's since the first letter of each of the original words in Japanese starts with the letter "s".

Benefits of implementing 5 S's?
- A better use of our resources, especially our time
- Make anomalies and problems visible and obvious
- Enjoy a safer and more pleasant work environment
- Increase our ability to produce more quality products
- Have a presentable place for our customers

When should we use it?
When we need to reduce cycle times by taking full advantage of the time available to produce and less time to change tooling. It is also useful when implementing new systems in the management of the value stream, such as ISO9000, statistical process control, Six Sigma, or Lean Manufacturing, since all of these depend to a great extent on the discipline of the people who participate.

This discipline is very powerful since it can be applied in every area:

- Warehouses
- Production areas
- Areas of common use
- Offices
- Workshops
- Vehicles
- Your own home

5 S's at home: A customer implemented 5 S's at home for his wine cellar and changing room. After moving into a new house more than 20 years ago, both rooms were quickly, but not effectively arranged. For years, the wine cellar was a dark, unorganized room with no space, no stock, and not a nice place to go and select wine. The changing room was basically a room full of clothes where you could barely move within it, it had insufficient lighting, and therefore he could not find the clothes he wanted. It took him more than 20 years to set up 5 S's, but now, the rooms are great, and he enjoys both. Actually, in the wine cellar he has regular wine tastings and get togethers.

Visual Management - Andon

Visual signals are all around us, such as on the streets, in companies, in hospitals, etc., to help us quickly understand a specific situation and be able to make decisions without having to ask someone.

We humans understand information through our different senses, with vision being the one with the highest perception at 83%, followed by the auditory at 11%, smell at 4%, and 2% for touch and taste.

Visual Management - Andon devices are simple visual and audio signals, which are easily identifiable and provide immediate and easy understanding. These signals are efficient, self-regulated, and handled by operators.

The signal may be used to identify or indicate that an abnormal condition exists and that action may be required.

Why implement Visual Management?
Andon signal elements are basically used to:

- Improve quality
- Reduce cost
- Improve response time
- Increase security
- Improve communication
- Provide immediate understanding of problems

How to decide what type of Visual Management?
When we use visual control, we must ask ourselves:

- What needs to be monitored?
- How to present it? Colors, size, content – use the KISS-Method
- Where are the critical monitoring points?
- How are abnormalities indicated?
- How easily can they be reviewed?
- What action should be taken?

Where can Visual Management be used?
- Warehouses
- Operating areas
- Equipment
- Quality
- Security

Types of Andon
1. Alarms
They provide information to give a warning signal in urgent situations and can be used with different sounds depending on their application.

2. Lamps and turrets

To display the state of the equipment, cells, or work areas, colored signals could be used in turrets or as flags that indicate the following:

- **Blue** = Problems related to supply or lack of material
- **Green** = Line or cell running satisfactorily
- **Yellow** = Line or cell stopped for lack of maintenance or that a change is about to be made if it is flashing
- **Red** = Stop due to quality problems or accidents

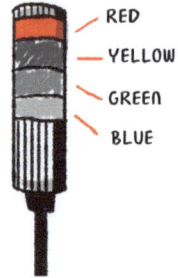

RED
YELLOW
GREEN
BLUE

3. Information Boards

These types of boards are useful for continuous and automatic monitoring of production in real time in order to compare the scheduled plan with the actual production level to identify if we are running at plan, faster, or slower.

They are also used when you want to visually highlight some operating condition in which a signal would draw the attention of the decision maker.

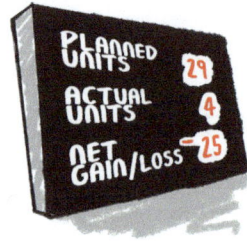

PLANNED UNITS 29
ACTUAL UNITS 4
NET GAIN/LOSS -25

Visual Management: In a medical device manufacturing company we were working with. Employees had different understanding of the vision, mission, values, strategy, Hoshin Kanri, the yearly and monthly goals but in particular they would not know how the company was doing day by day and how they would have achieved the monthly targets. We felt like a plane without instruments and trying to be at the right height and speed to reach a destination on time.. There was barely no information available for employees, even though we would ask them to help to improve numbers and processes. A communication center (in the middle of the plant) was set up by an interdisciplinary team, with all relevant information all employees had to know. After a couple months all relevant meetings (all standing) would be held in the area, in front of the resp. information boards. The Information center would have all relevant boards like: Customer VOC, Marketing & Sales, Quality, Supply Chain, Value Streams, Maintenance, Key Projects, HR. It became the central point for the whole plant where all relevant information was up to date at any time and key decision could be taken at any time.

How to implement Visual Management?

Andon can be implemented as an Improvement Cycle and will help to avoid corrective actions in the future.

1. Decide what information needs to be given and to whom it is addressed
2. Create the type of Andon or signal that is necessary
3. Train staff in the use of this tool
4. Create discipline with good leadership to enforce the signals

Standardized Work

Standardized work is based on operational excellence. Without standardized work, it is not possible to guarantee that the operation will always produce products in the same way. Standardized work makes it possible to apply the elements of Lean Manufacturing because it defines the most efficient working methods to achieve the best quality and lowest cost.

To understand standard work, we need to have the following elements clearly defined:

1. Speed of process
2. Correct sequence
3. Key points established
4. Explanation of reasons for key points

Why standard work is so important?

By standardizing operations, the baseline is established to evaluate and manage the processes and evaluate their performance, which will be the basis for the improvements. The standard working documentation serves to:

- Ensure that the sequence of operator actions is repeatable
- Support visual control, detecting abnormalities
- Provide help comparing documentation with current processes
- Be a tool to initiate improvement actions
- Facilitate documentation method of improvements
- Establish an invaluable database of information
- Help maintain a high level of repeatability
- Ensure safer and more effective operations
- Improve productivity
- Help to balance the cycle times of all operations according to the takt time cycle
- Reduce the learning curve of operators

When is it used?

It is used to document relevant processes and to train personnel.

Procedure for carrying it out
- Select a specific process or process operation
- Make the corresponding time measurements and capture them in the attached time-stamp format
- Calculate the operating capacity and fill the capacity format
- Design or document the optimized sequence of capacity in the "Combined Table"
- Draw the process on the "standard worksheet"
- Document the working instructions on the relevant sheet

Poka Yoke

Translation from Japanese

Poka = unnoticed errors   **Yoke** = avoid

Traditionally, in order to insure the desired quality level, many sophisticated statistical controls and sampling methods were implemented, which cost the company a great deal of money and valuable time.

Poka Yoke is a method to avoid human errors in processes before they become defects and makes it possible for operators to concentrate on their activities. It allows 100% detection and immediate corrective action when defects appear without using statistical methods.

KEY PRINCIPLE
Error is inevitable, but it should be eliminated

Examples of Sources of Defects and Reworks

Materials	Workforce	Methods	Machinery
Damaged	Lack of training	Incomplete	Inadequate maintenance
Wrong	Mistakes	Obsolete	Incorrect operation
Out of spec.	Neglect	Complex	Not installed properly
Obsolete	Sabotage		

In Lean Manufacturing, a very important rule to consider is the fact that no operation or step sends defective products to the next operation because the continuous flow is interrupted.

Some of the applications and benefits of applying Poka Yoke are:
- Ensures quality in each job
- Provides knowledge to the people responsible for performing a task
- Eliminates or reduce the possibility of making mistakes
- Avoids accidents caused by human distraction
- Eliminates actions that depend on memory and inspection
- Frees the mind of the worker, allowing him to develop his creativity
- Usually cheap and simple

Types of Poke Yoke

- Warning Poka Yoke: The warning element warns the operator or user before the error can occur. However, the warning does not necessarily mean that the error will be avoided.
- Prevention Poka Yoke: This type of element, seeks that errors do not occur by using mechanisms that make it impossible to make the error.

Effective Levels of Poka Yoke
1. Detects the defect when it has already occurred, and generally ensures that it does not reach the next station.
2. Detects the error when it occurs and before it becomes a defect.
3. Eliminates or prevents the generation of errors before they occur and cause defects.

Examples of Poka Yoke Devices
- Guide pin
- Template
- Microswitch/switch limit
- Counter
- Dispenser
- Sequence device
- Critical condition indicator
- Sensors and detectors
- Color code

Poka Yoke: An auto parts company wanted to increase the inspection team and buy a piece of expensive high-tech equipment in order to measure diameters with a gauge due to continuous rejections and re-works from their customer. After a thorough review. a Lean Six Sigma team suggested using a Poka Yoke tool, implementing 100% inspection of the product during production by using two types of simple gauges to measure diameters, which simulated what the customer was actually doing at his facility.

By implementing this simple go-no-go gauge, the company saved 45,000 USD in expense for the equipment plus the inspectors' salaries, while guaranteeing continual excellent quality. The existing operator now performs a simple verification step by testing 100% of the units before they perform their operation. The cost of the go no-go gauges was less than 2,500 USD The customer is happy due to a continual excellent quality, and the company saved money, time and costs of additional operators.

3.4 PROBLEM SOLVING A3 AND ISHIKAWA DIAGRAM

A3 is a structured problem solving and continuous improvement approach and was first implemented at Toyota. It provides a simple and strict approach to systematically lead towards problem solving with structured approaches.

It is called A3 because it was originally done on an A3 single sheet of paper.

The process how to lead through an A3 problem solving process is based on the principles of Edward Deming's PDCA.

Process:

The A3 Process is usually divided into 7 Steps:

1. Background Information/Problem Description
2. Current Condition/Problem Clarification (5 W's)
3. Goal/Target Condition
4. Root Cause Analysis (Ishikawa)
5. Proposed Counter Measures
6. Plan
7. Follow-up and Review

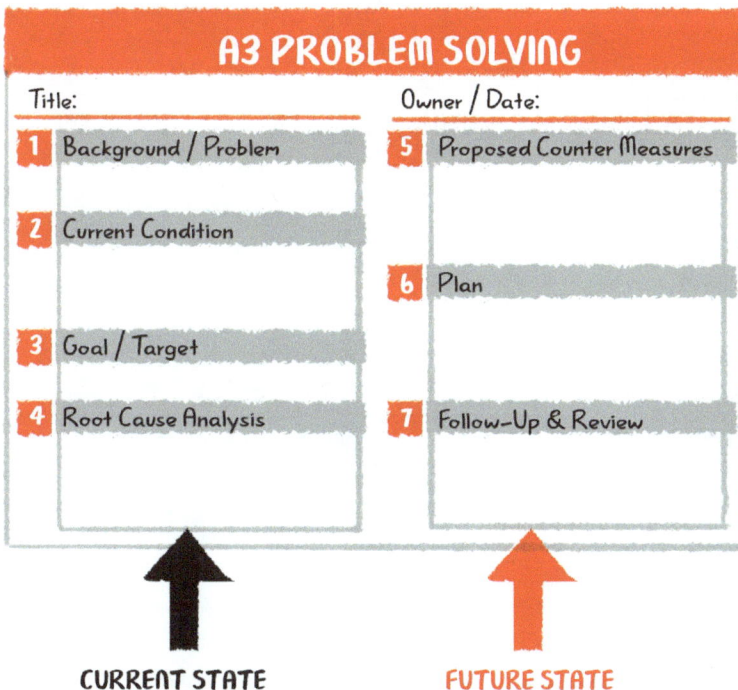

A3 PROBLEM SOLVING

Title: Owner / Date:

1 Background / Problem   5 Proposed Counter Measures

2 Current Condition

                                  6 Plan

3 Goal / Target

4 Root Cause Analysis   7 Follow-Up & Review

CURRENT STATE   FUTURE STATE

The A3-Process is a great way to systematically solve a problem, document the process, keep the whole team up to date, and inform who is doing what by when. From Points 1-4 on the left side of the A3-format, we record the Current Situation of the problem, and on the right side from Points 5-7, we record the Future State and actions.

Learn more in the LSSM – Fieldbook

Fishbone or Ishikawa Diagrams *Also called Cause and Effect Diagrams.*

Common uses of Ishikawa

Common uses of Ishikawa diagrams are product design and quality defect prevention to identify potential factors causing an overall effect. Each cause or reason is a source of variation. Causes are usually grouped into major categories to identify and classify these sources of variation.

The 5 M's used in manufacturing

Originating with lean manufacturing and the Toyota Production System, 5 M's is one of the most common frameworks for root-cause analysis:
- Machines (equipment)
- Methods (process)
- Materials (raw material, consumables, and information)
- Manpower (physical or knowledge work)
- Measurement (inspection, environment)

Sometimes expanded with:
- Management (money, power, leadership)
- Maintenance
- Mission (purpose, environment)

THE FISHBONE DIAGRAM

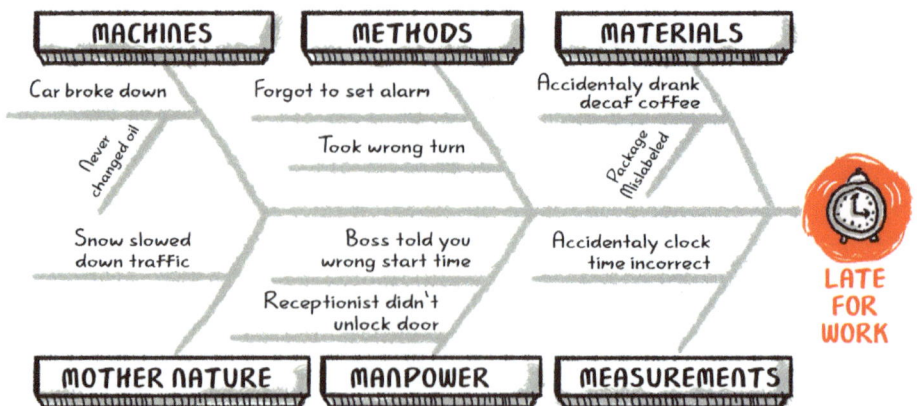

MACHINES	METHODS	MATERIALS
Car broke down	Forgot to set alarm	Accidentaly drank decaf coffee
Never changed oil	Took wrong turn	Package Mislabeled
Snow slowed down traffic	Boss told you wrong start time	Accidentaly clock time incorrect
	Receptionist didn't unlock door	
MOTHER NATURE	MANPOWER	MEASUREMENTS

LATE FOR WORK

Process of an Ishikawa Diagram

1. Define the effect of the problem (such as late for work)
2. Brainstorm with a multidisciplinary team for each "bone"— Equipment, Process, People, Materials, Environment, and Management for potential root cause
3. Be specific and open minded; don't finger point about who could have caused the problem
4. After the brainstorming, try to group potential causes
5. Validate each root cause — how likely is this cause to be the major source of the issue or variation?
6. After excluding all non-likely causes, keep the ones you consider important to review close
7. The V causes need to be investigated further, so an action plan is created for corrective and preventive actions
8. After implementing a CAPA Plan (Corrective - Preventive Action Plan), revalidate that the problem has been fixed and the CAPA can be closed

Learn more in the LSSM - Fieldbook

3.5 PREVENTION METHOD - FMEA

The discipline of Failure Mode and Effect Analysis was developed in 1949 in the United States by the military as PMIL-STD-1629A, titled "Procedure for the Execution of a Mode of Failure, Effects and Criticality Analysis."

FMEA was used in the aerospace industry for the Apollo Program in the mid-60's.

The analysis of the mode and the effect of the faults was used as a technique to evaluate the reliability and effects of failures of equipment and systems, on the success of the mission, and the safety of personnel or equipment.

FMEA is a risk management tool that identifies and prevents faults in products and processes, objectively evaluates their effect, causes, and elements of detection to avoid their occurrence, and provides a documented method of prevention.

The FMEA process and documents are highly valuable, living documents that can help us to store a large amount of information about our processes and products. This makes them a very powerful tool.

Types of FMEA's

- **Product:** It serves to detect possible failures in the design of products
- **Process:** It serves to detect posible failures in any type of process

Every process should have its own FMEA to anticipate any risk or potential failure. Therefore processes such as human resources, product design, sales, marketing, logistics, procurement, service, manufacturing, maintenance, quality, and accounting should be evaluated.

Benefits of FMEA's
- Understand the details of any process
- Include the information as a basis for operations training
- Identify possible failures in a process or product
- Establish the effects of each failure if one should happen
- Evaluate the level of severity of the effects
- Identify the possible cause
- Establish the reliability level of our fault detection mechanisms
- Objectively evaluate the relationship of severity, occurrence, and detectability
- Document actions to reduce risks
- Understand the mechanics that create defects and faults
- Save the knowledge generated in a company
- Be a source of detection of opportunities to initiate improvement projects

When is it needed?
- In the design of products or services
- In the design of processes
- To avoid the occurrence of problems or failures
- To document the processes and products
- To train operators in a process

Implementation time
- A FMEA normally takes 1 - 4 days to initiate
- Procedure to develop an FMEA
- Develop the process map
- Form a work team and document the process, product, etc.
- Choose the critical steps of the process.
- Determine potential failure of each step
- Define the effects of the failures
- Evaluate their level of severity
- Indicate the causes of each failure
- Evaluate the occurrence of each failure
- Indicate the controls that are supposed to detect faults and evaluate them
- Calculate the priority number for each failure
- Develop preventive, corrective, or improvement actions

Learn more to in the LSSM - Fieldbook

3.6 CONTINUOUS FLOW – ONE PIECE FLOW

In 1776, Adam Smith, Scottish economist and philosopher, showed that the division of labor into specific jobs would result in increased productivity. This concept was supported by Frederic Taylor, the father of scientific management, ensuring that the work of specialists dedicated to repetitive tasks would result in more productive work.

With the application of production lines by Henry Ford, greater emphasis was given to the idea of specializing the work and making it go through long assembly lines. Currently, the conditions of demand and volume have changed from large lots of the same product to small lots with great variety, which makes it impossible to continue working the same way. That is why Lean Manufacturing proposes, from the first applications in Toyota by Shigeo Shingo, that work be done in continuous flow.

The cellular concept of "work cell" proposes the elimination of large lots that are manufactured in each department to prevent the production from being stopped in any of these areas. We are introducing a continuous flow from the first to the last operation.

U-SHAPED CELL

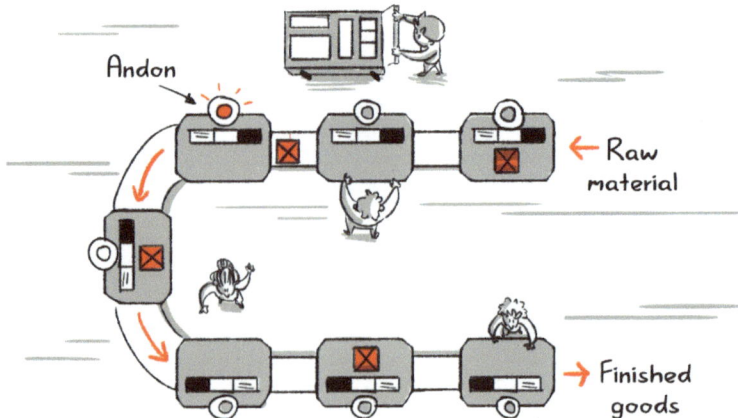

Continuous flow or cellular work is a concept in which the distribution of operations is significantly improved by flowing the process uninterruptedly from one operation to the next operation, drastically reducing response time and maximizing personnel skills and performance. Inventory will also be reduced to an absolute minimum.

Layout of manufacturing by departments present the following problems:
- Defects are not detected until the service is performed or the product is finished
- Some of the defects are generated by handling or moving materials or people
- People spend too much time waiting between each stage of the process
- Inventories of materials or long queues sometimes occupy as much as 25% of the total space

Continuous flow will help to:
- Improve teamwork and communication - employees are now close enough to each other and can be supported if necessary
- A complete understanding of the whole process
- An opportunity to meet your customers and discuss with them any concept or development
- An environment where workers have a greater sense of responsibility and control of their activities
- Responsibility and ownership of producing products or services with high quality from the first time
- Greater satisfaction in the work since it increases the responsibility and the variety

One-piece flow: A metal/plastics manufacturing company was producing in batches and needed to increase efficiency, quality, and reduce inventories in their processes. The team started a one-week Kaizen event in order to define the plan to start one-piece flow in the whole company. After one week, everything was planned and prepared to start with a pilot in one cell. However, more preparation was needed to train and certify the personnel. After one year approximately, 50% of the manufacturing lines were set up in one-piece flow with a 28% gain in productivity and 80% better first yield. Scrap was reduced from 18% down to 12%. No one was let go because the employees that were not required anymore were moved to another manufacturing line. In addition, inventories were reduced by 70%!

3.7 TPM - TOTAL PRODUCTIVE MAINTENANCE

Total Productive Maintenance (TPM) has its origins in the United States, where many manufacturing companies applied certain practices to prevent failures and thereby prevent untimely stoppages and emergency repairs. In the postwar period, as Japan rebuilt its economy, several Japanese managers and engineers visited these plants to take ideas and implement them in Japan.

It was at Nippondenso, a Toyota auto parts factory, where maintenance concepts were applied for the first-time by involving all employees of the organization (not just maintenance specialists). Special emphasis was placed on the implementation of practices in which operators were responsible for the maintenance and care of the conditions of operation and maintenance of their equipment. That is why the company won the prize for the most distinguished plant by the Japanese Institute of Plant Maintenance for the first time in 1971. It was then when Seiichi Nakajima published a description of the process of implementing this system, the elements that compose it, and the way in which it should be implemented. In 1987, the historic circle closed when this system returned to its homeland, with Kodak being the first company to implement TPM in the U.S.

The cost of equipment losses

Usually, for every 300 hundred unattended minor problems, such as lack of cleanliness, lubrication, etc. 30 medium problems are generated and from these, one major problem occurs, such as an expensive component replacement.

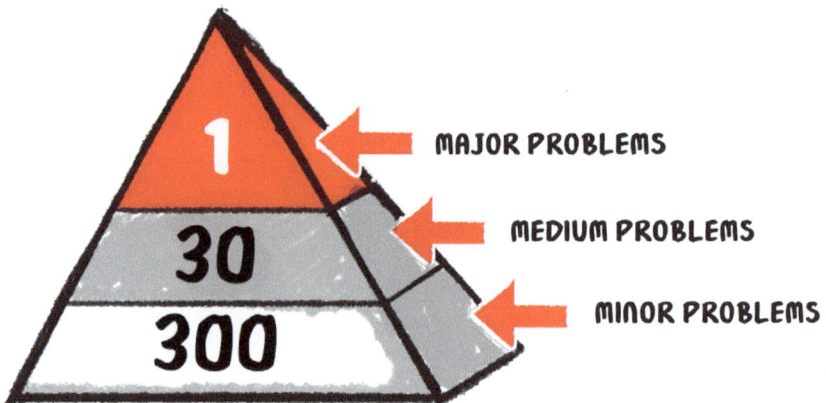

Maintenance costs

- Maintenance costs may represent between 15% to 40% of total manufacturing costs
- Emergency repairs cost at least three times more than if the same repairs had been planned
- 58% of the cost of maintenance is caused by poor operation
- 17% of the cost of maintenance is caused by poor lubrication

These are amazing numbers we need to prevent!

Total Productive Maintenance is an improvement methodology that allows the continuity of any operation through the following concepts:
1. Prevention
2. Zero defects
3. Zero accidents
4. Total participation of all employees

In manufacturing companies, the maintenance of machines usually represents a latent problem of potential downtime and stoppage.

Current Challenges

In traditional companies, personal care and maintenance are not a priority and thus resources are generally not allocated for:

- Developing care and awareness programs
- Formulating an appropriate plan of maintenance and upkeep
- Providing adequate preventive and predictive maintenance
- Training users in basic care

- Developing maintenance professionals
- Buying supplies required for proper maintenance
- Having the necessary tools to do the job

The truth is that the process cannot be allowed to stop delivering value to the customer due to lack of personnel or equipment. So, when people and equipment fail, large amounts of money and time have to be spent to return the continuity of the process. People who work in maintenance suffer great stress because they spend more time troubleshooting and repairing than planning and improving facilities. The reality is that in many cases, they have fallen into a vicious cycle of failure and repairing equipment when there is a lack of assigning priorities according to the level of the complaints of those in need.

The 6 Pillars of Total Productive Maintenance
1. Continuous improvement
2. Autonomous maintenance
3. Planned Maintenance
4. Quality Maintenance
5. Training
6. Safety

Total Productive Maintenance Benefits

The main benefit is to maintain in optimum condition all the factors that are required by the business to ensure continuity in the delivery of value. The following are additional benefits:

- Achieve the maximum potential of the facilities and equipment
- Significantly reduce risks
- Improve the quality of products or services
- Ensure the integrity of the people with the highest safety
- Reduce costs associated with repairs, breakdowns, downtime, etc.
- Maximize the effectiveness of the company
- Increase the lifespan of equipment
- Eliminate forced wear and tear
- Remove the six big losses of equipment
- Reduce energy consumption

The 6 big losses of a Team
1. Breakdowns – lost time when equipment is stopped for repairs
2. Dead time when equipment is stopped for changeovers or setups
3. Minor injuries
4. Speed reductions due to adjustments, failures, or not running at a constant speed
5. Time spent producing defects during the production process
6. Defects produced while equipment is warming up after changeover or adjustment

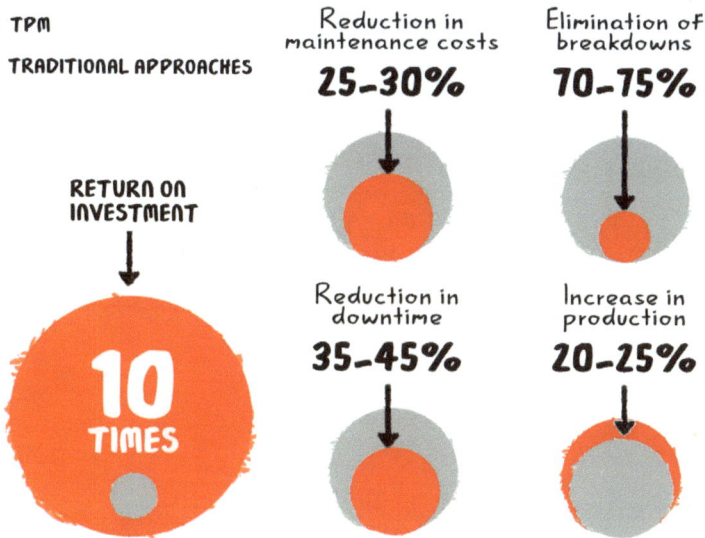

TPM

TRADITIONAL APPROACHES

RETURN ON INVESTMENT

10 TIMES

Reduction in maintenance costs
25-30%

Elimination of breakdowns
70-75%

Reduction in downtime
35-45%

Increase in production
20-25%

Overall Equipment Effectiveness (OEE)

This measurement is critical to evaluate the actual capacity to produce without defects to the potential capacity without defects. It is necessary to obtain the data every day to be able to perform the following calculations:

- **Availability (B/A)** = (Time Available - Timeout)/Available Time
- **Efficiency (D/C)** = Total production/(Operating Time x Capacity)
- **Quality (F/E)** (Total Production - Defects and Retracted)/Total Production
- **OEE** = Availability x Efficiency x Quality

TOTAL OPERATIONS

				Unscheduled
AVAILABILITY	A Potential production time			
	B Actual production time		Time loss: - Breakdowns, Waiting	
PERFORMANCE	C Theorectical output			
	D Actual output	Speed loss: - Minor stoppages - Reduced speed	Loss of Effectiveness	
QUALITY	E Actual output			
	F Good product output	Quality loss: - Scrap - Rework		
OEE - availability rate x performance rate x quality rate : B/A x D/C x F/E				

117

In general, OEE with the following percentages are:

< 45%	Poor
50% - 64%	Average
65% - 74%	Good
75% - 84%	Very good
> 85%	Excellent – world class

The goal is to increase the OEE through an Efficiency increase. This can be achieved through reduction of breakdowns, waiting, minor stoppages, reduced speeds, and reduction of scrap, rework.

TPM: A metal/plastics manufacturing company had a problem of late deliveries and quality complaints from their customers. The bottleneck was a forming machine that had the most downtime. The machine was selected for a pilot project where TPM was implemented. They started with a super cleaning event and implemented autonomous maintenance by giving the operator the task of cleaning and lubricating the machine every day, as well as, designing a preventive and predictive plan for the maintenance department. After the pilot phase, the machine was put back into regular operation, and the results were amazing. From the 60% downtime they had previously, they achieved less than 10% after three months. As a result, deliveries and quality improved to the point that they reached 4-Sigma level.

In the LSSM - Fieldbook, we will go through more OEE examples and exercise, including several simple to use formats.

3.8 SMED - QUICK CHANGE OVER

Taiichi Ohno, head of production at Toyota, analyzed very carefully how the U.S. auto industry worked back in the 1960's, when they had many presses to be able to manufacture parts for different models and not have to change the molds, because in some cases, the changeover would take them more than 24 hours. On the other hand, Toyota had a limited number of presses, so the challenge was to manufacture a wide range of vehicles with a much smaller amount of equipment. Shigeo Shingo was hired as a consultant, and with his guidance, Toyota was making changes to presses of over 1,000 tons in almost three minutes by 1970.

Quick Preparation is also known as "Single Minute Exchange of Die" (SMED) or Quick Change Over. Shigeo Shingo is the creator of SMED and other lean applications. Quick Change Over is important because many activities in life depend on how fast we can start an activity or how fast we can configure our process to change a product or service. For example, when a surgery is finished, imagine all activities that need to happen before the next surgery starts (cleaning, waste disposals, disinfection, prepare instruments, close all the documents for the previous surgery, get the new documents ready, calibrate equipment, etc.)

Another example of a Quick Change Over is a pit stop for a car race: change tires, refuel, check, calibrate, clean, etc. In the past, the team needed several minutes; then, it was reduced to one minute, 30 seconds, 10 seconds, and today, only two seconds!

The goal of a quick Change Over is to drastically reduce the time that it takes to go from one operation to the next. In other words, the goal is to reduce the cash flow cycle time. The reduction in changeover time helps the company produce a greater variety of items (colors and sizes, for example) or services, using the same equipment or the same areas in a shorter amount of time.

Quick Change Overs will significantly reduce:
- Timeouts
- Customer Complaints and Defects
- Delivery time
- Work in progress
- Inventory of finished product
- Investment in parts (materials, spare parts)

Quick Change Overs will provide:
- Best inventory rotation
- Improvements in productivity
- Increase in capacity
- Greater flexibility in the face of demand

SMED in a restaurant: Imagine that you are waiting in a queue to be seated for more than 10 minutes. When you look around, there are actually many empty tables available, but they need to be cleaned and set up. The best-in-class SMED for restaurants we have seen in Brazil, where a table for 6-8 people is cleaned, prepared, and set up in less than 8 seconds. Actually, you would not have reached the exit door to leave when the table is ready for the next guests. This helps people coming into the restaurant to get seated rapidly.

SMED Improvement Cycle

When we have determined that the bottleneck in the system requires a drastic reduction in preparation time, then, we conduct a Kaizen event for shortening the changeover/setup to improve overall productivity.

Planning
- Perform a Value Stream Map of the service or manufacturing process
- Determine the impact of doing a Kaizen Improvement Preparation Time Event
- Select the equipment or service to improve changeover time. It is important to focus on the bottleneck

- Establish a multidisciplinary team of people from diverse areas, such as production operators, quality and maintenance personnel, etc.
- Check the production schedule to set a start date for the Kaizen Event
- Get a video camera to use in order to be able to review the actual process
- Introduce the Quick Changes theme for the Kaizen team staff

Execution
- Observe and measure total changeover time
- Separate activities that are done during the preparation and turn them into activities outside the preparation
- Convert internal activities to external activities and move the external activities out of preparation
- Eliminate waste in internal activities
- Eliminate waste from external activities
- Standardize and maintain the new procedure

Follow-up
In the last stage of the improvement, a very clear and simple procedure or instruction should be established to carry out the change and a checklist prepared to ensure that the achievements obtained in the application of the methodology are maintained and performed consistently.

- Document improved change procedures
- Communicate with everyone involved
- Train the people involved in the change
- Provide standardized work instructions at workplaces
- Set a goal for the changes
- Measure, publish and track change times

3.9 KANBAN

In the 1970's, Taiichi Ohno, head of operations at Toyota, and his colleagues visited some automotive plants and other types of manufacturing plants in the U.S. to look for a scheduling system that would prevent producing high levels of inventory.

They did not find what they were looking for at the plants, but when they visited supermarkets during their trip, they were attracted by the way in which the items were restocked once the customer removed them from the shelf. When payment at the cash register was completed, a signal was sent to the supplier indicating that he needed to restock the product(s) that the customer had purchased.

The Kanban system has been developed based on the way supermarkets work, where money or payment is a signal to replenish the goods in shelves. Therefore, the Kanban system has been set up with cards to symbolize the money.

A Kanban is a card that identifies the items, controls the flow of the items, and documents the results.

A Pull system is a communication system that allows production control, synchronizes manufacturing processes with customer requirements, and strongly supports production scheduling.

Types of Kanban

Withdrawal Kanban

Specifies the type and quantity of product a process should withdraw from the previous process.

Indicates the type and quantity of products
that a process should withdraw from the previous process

STORAGE RACK #	F26-18	PART CODE	A5-34	
PART #	56690-321		**PREVIOUS PROCESS**	
NAME OF THE PART	MOTOR SUPPORT		STAMP B-2	
BOX CAPACITY	TYPE OF BOX		**NEXT PROCESS**	
20	B		MECHANIZATION	

Production Kanban

Specifies the type and quantity of product a process must produce.
In the next figure, you can see how the Kanban works. First, the operator withdraws product A, then, the empty space or card (Kanban) will notify the operator to replenish the item A to make it available for the next customer.

Indicates the type and quantity
of products a process should produce

STORAGE RACK #	F26-18	PART CODE	A5-34
PART #	56690-321		
NAME OF THE PART	MOTOR SUPPORT		
QUANTITY TO PRODUCE	200	**PROCESS**	
		MECHANIZATION	

EMPTY SPACE IS A SIGNAL TO REPLACE THE MISSING "A"

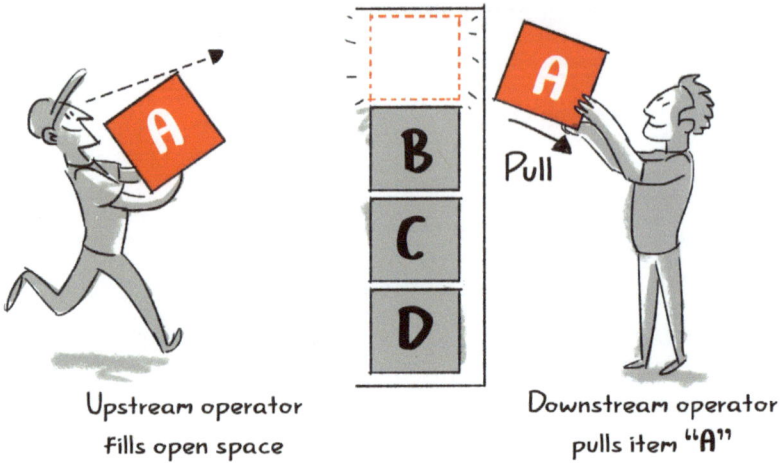

Upstream operator fills open space

Pull

Downstream operator pulls item "A"

Kanban Rules
- Do not pass defective products to the following processes
- A Kanban is removed when a process removes parts from the previous process
- Each manufacturing process produces the quantities specified by the retired Kanban (the Kanban provides the production order)
- Nothing is produced or transported without Kanban
- Kanban makes the function of a production order attached to the items
- The number of Kanban's decreases with time

Kanban: A pharmaceutical company implemented cellular manufacturing, TPM, SMED and other tools, but they kept their unreliable MRP system to plan production orders. This was a nightmare because they changed the manufacturing plan every day due to incorrect scheduling. This created higher and higher inventories at the plant and delivery delays to the customer. We helped them to implement a Kanban system, develop a pull production system, and release production orders only when they were needed. This created a smooth flow and reduced inventories from 4.5 months to less than 30 days in less than six months!

Please refer to LSSM - Fieldbook to learn about an example of pull system application.

3.10 SIX SIGMA

Six Sigma is the result of the evolution of quality systems through the development of management by total quality that describes a philosophy that converts quality values into the greatest strength behind leadership, design, planning, execution, and improvement. The discipline of quality is much more than rules and awards, it's a system of knowledge and execution that involves constantly improving the way we work.

William Deming, Joseph Juran, Philip B. Crosby, Armand V. Feigenbaum, Kaoru Ishikawa, Genichi Taguchi and many others contributed their effort and dedication to forging what is now known as the concept and philosophy of quality. They introduced the premises for what is now known as Six Sigma.

In the 1980's, Motorola was experiencing a crisis of competitiveness where its results did not project a promising outlook. Bob Galvin, Chief Executive Officer (CEO) of the company, once said "our quality stinks." The problem was that the quality level was so low that it could cause the closure of the company. So, he ordered his staff to significantly improve the quality level, seeking to advance from 3 Sigma Level (93.3% of good products) to a 4 Sigma Level (99.3%). The quality increased significantly and continued to reach a Six Sigma Level, which means only 3.4 defects per million opportunities (products or services).

Several company engineers that began working towards quality, especially Mikel Harry, caught the attention of Galvin by proposing to stop using the average as a way to evaluate overall performance. They proposed that standard deviation would be better since when it was measured, it represented the variation of a set of data with respect to its mean. This would be more important to consistently measure the quality of products rather than averaging good and bad results.

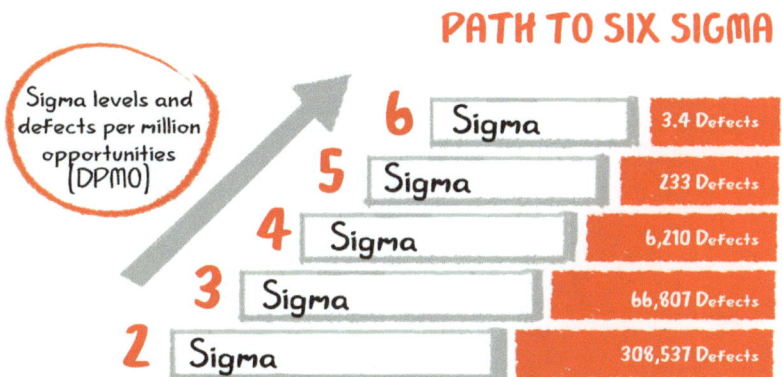

PATH TO SIX SIGMA

Sigma levels and defects per million opportunities (DPMO)		
6 Sigma	3.4 Defects
5 Sigma	233 Defects
4 Sigma	6,210 Defects
3 Sigma	66,807 Defects
2 Sigma	308,537 Defects

In the United States, Malcolm Baldridge, who was Secretary of Commerce from 1981 to 1987, presented a proposal to President Ronald Reagan to establish a National Quality Award. Shortly before the award was given for the first time, Secretary Baldridge died in a car accident. Afterward, the award was named after him as the Malcom Baldridge National Quality Award. In 1988, Motorola received this award for not only achieving of 4 Sigma level, but for bringing some processes up to the almost perfect quality level of 99.9996%, equivalent to Six Sigma. In 2010, the award's name was changed to the Baldrige Performance Excellence Program.

Other companies such as General Electric, Lockheed Martin, Texas Instruments, Honeywell, followed the example of Motorola and continued the development of their personnel and their projects in favor of a more efficient and productive industry.

"Six Sigma is a quality program that, when all is said and done, improves your customers' experience, lowers your costs, and builds better leaders." **Jack Welch, CEO of General Electric.**

Six Sigma has several definitions

1. It is a metric that allows measuring any process and comparing it with another.
2. It is an improvement methodology that serves to drastically reduce the variation.
3. It is a management system to achieve business leadership and maximum performance.

When the variations are statistically measured, they are the dispersion of a set of data with respect to its mean, and the Greek letter sigma is used to identify the standard deviation.

SIGMA LEVEL	DEFECTS PER MILLION	DEFECTS PERCENTAGE
1	691,462	69%
2	308,538	31%
3	66,807	6.7%
4	6,210	0.62%
5	233	0.023%
6	3.4	0.00034%
7	0.019	0.0000019%

Why implement Six Sigma?

Some of the applications and benefits of applying Six Sigma are:

- Ensure quality in every job
- Create a base of people capable of improving quality
- Establish a work philosophy and a business strategy
- Improve the quality of products and services significantly
- Ensure the permanence of the business
- Increase profitability
- Develop robust products and processes
- Ensure a clear understanding of customer requirements

Six Sigma is used when we want to reduce the variability in the processes, improve the level of compliance with the client's specifications when they show a variation that has gone out of control, or when quality levels do not meet customer expectations and the existing variation forces better process performance.

Six Sigma Tools
- Project plan
- Quality Function deployment
- Kano Model
- Sampling
- Gauge R&R
- Histogram
- Capability analysis
- Hypothesis testing and confidence intervals
- Descriptive statistics
- Design of experiments
- Regression analysis
- Statistical control

Characteristics of Six Sigma
- A training structure is established
- The application approach is proactive
- A structured methodology is used with diverse tools
- Focuses on working on key process variables
- The principle is to work on the critical characteristics of quality
- Quality is generated in processes and not in inspections
- Outputs of processes are dependent on inputs

Relationship of Six Sigma with Lean Manufacturing

Some experts estimate that a company that has 10% waste, can reduce up to 40% of its capacity. That is why speed (lean) and quality (Six Sigma) are opposite faces of the same coin.

If we speak about agile companies, it requires not only a methodology for improvement and a set of methods that help us reduce defects, improve delivery speed, and therefore customer satisfaction.

In this book, we have suggested methodologies and their tools to create agile companies. These methodologies work well when given the necessary focus. We have described the following functions.

Methodology Application:
In Lean Six Sigma, we use the Six Sigma methodology and a combination of lean and statistical tools.

Six Sigma Methodology DMAIC
   1. **Define**
   2. **Measure**
   3. **Analyze**
   4. **Improve**
   5. **Control**

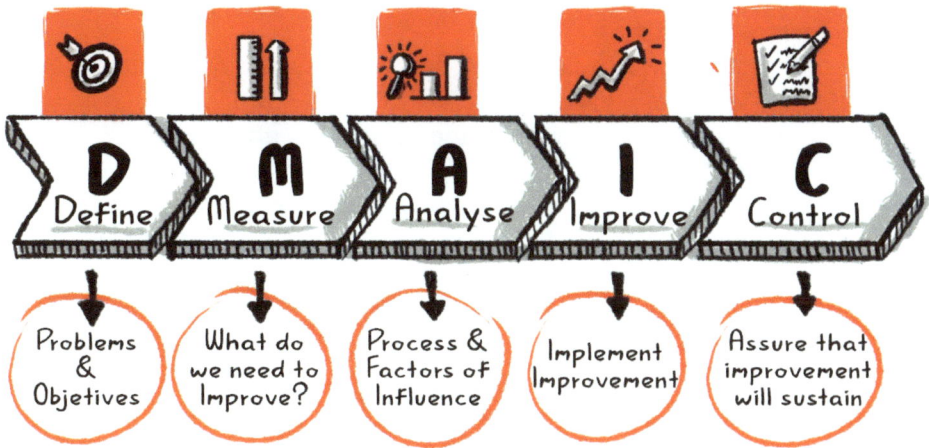

For Innovation, the methodology is called **DMADV** for:
1. **Define**
2. **Measure**
3. **Analyze**
4. **Design**
5. **Validate**

In both cases, Lean Six Sigma uses the above described methodologies with Lean and Six Sigma tools.

In the LSSM – Fieldbook, we explain how the different phases will be implemented step by step.

3.11 KEY POINTS

1. Choose the tools that will be most easily understood and effective for your company.
2. Select a methodology to support the company´s philosophy.
3. Prepare people from all company levels as white belts, yellow belts, green belts, black belts. and Master Black Belts to practice continual improvement cycles using the right combination of tools as needed.
4. Kaizen and Kaikaku are terrific tools to improve a process.
5. Start implementing simple and basic tools like 5 S's, Andon, Standard Work, or Poka Yoke.
6. Doing a thorough FMEA will prevent future failures.
7. Use A3 to document problem solving and an Ishikwa Diagram to find the root cause.
8. Continuous Flow will help reduce all types of inefficiencies like inventories, waiting time, defects, scrap, while increasing speed in the line and improving communication.
9. TPM and OEE help improve efficiency and becoming best-in-class in the industry.
10. SMED is the tool to reduce change over time to make happen in seconds what needed hours in the past.
11. Kanban helps to keep inventories at a low level and never be missing parts when you need them.
12. Six Sigma is a statistical process in order to decrease defects per million pieces. Airlines and some other industries have shown that a process can be at 7 or 8 Sigma level, which is below one defect per million pieces.
13. The combination of Lean and Six Sigma is the perfect combination and every business should strive for it.

Please add your own Key Points:

_____
_____
_____
_____
_____
_____
_____
_____
_____
_____
_____

CHAPTER 4

4. GETTING STARTED AND TRANSFORM TO A LEAN SIX SIGMA COMPANY

4.1 HOW WILL COMPANIES OF THE FUTURE BE DESIGNED?

Now that we have reviewed all the key tools, we are ready to get started. Some of us may have started multiple times, some have just started, and some have not started yet. Don't worry. We will guide you how to start and be successful.

Always start with the end in mind. This means to ask yourself: How do I want my company to be after the transformation? What needs to change? What do I want to keep? What needs to be done less, and what needs to stop in order to transform into a Lean Six Sigma Company?

Lean Six Sigma companies include the following elements:

- **Strategy:** It is helpful to have a clear destination and the path the company should follow to achieve its goals for customers, shareholders, employees, and society.

- **Structure:** The design of the organizational structure is critical for companies that evolve faster than their competition around the value created for customers. The structure is very simple and agile because now the responsibility does not fall on individual people, but on the following teams:

- **Management Team:** Formed by the CEO and managers of the value stream who have the responsibility of creating the strategy, communicating it, defining objectives, and continually measuring them to make decisions for the whole company.

- **Value Stream Teams:** All employees assigned to the processes that generate value for the customer; that is, all the people in sales, design, engineering, logistics, production and/or service, quality, maintenance, etc. needed to bring a product or service from material to finished good or service to the customers. It is intended that they work and are evaluated as a team, not as belonging to separate departments. The leader of the value stream now has the responsibility and authority for the overall process.

- **Process Teams:** Each team develops their daily work, making sure the generation of value never stops. To do this, the teams make sure that all process conditions are met. Some process teams may be serving on more than one value stream. Example. Accounting for the generation of the profit and loss statement for the entire company.

- **Improvement Implementation Team:** These are teams formed with Lean Six Sigma experts dedicated to implementing improvements or solving complex problems. It is very important to dedicate specific people to the transformation.

- **Talent Development:** The design of the way in which people should be hired, developed, and evaluated largely determines the successful operation of the whole company since the entire system functions through people and the talent they possess.

- **Processes of a Value Stream:** Lean Company only works if the processes that make up the value stream have the same focus and leadership. The priority of all, as a single team, will eliminate all forms of waste, hardship, and variability. To do this, each person designs new ways to do their work with a focus on the value stream.

The processes to consider are:

- **Product Design:** The research and development process is designed to eliminate waste and use statistical tools and creativity to accelerate the launching the product to the market, introduce the product to manufacturing more efficiently, achieve the target cost, and develop products with better quality and satisfaction for the customer.

- **Marketing:** The design of the marketing and sales processes is strongly focused on expanding our market when we have the available capacity and need to increase sales, reduce costs, and develop more customers committed to our brand. This is done with an emphasis on the satisfaction and value creation for the customer.

- **Logistics:** The functions of planning, purchasing, warehousing, and shipping are designed to eliminate any waste and link the supply chain with suppliers and customers, that is, making the process to obtain available materials and information flow to add customer value.

- **Manufacturing:** Design and development operations are performed using cell manufacturing and self-directed teams with people from different processes that make the material and product flow without interruption and with the best quality in order to deliver maximum customer value at the target cost.

- **Service:** In service companies, teams are designed to perform services using multiple skills in a continuous flow without interruptions to respond in the shortest time possible to create a true experience of satisfaction to customers receiving the service.

- **Accounting:** In a Lean Six Sigma Company, the process flow and money flow are fully interconnected. This is why we should design an accounting and financial process that permits making the best decisions for each value stream and the company, making collection processes, payables, budgets, presentation of results, etc. more agile and effective with the same focus on value.

- **Quality:** The process is designed so that quality is built into the processes that add value to the customer, not necessarily in a department of the company. Quality systems are developed by unifying all elements of each process of the value stream.

- **Maintenance:** Delivering value should never stop because some equipment, facility, or system is not working. Maintenance has become critical and is no longer a forgotten process in companies. Virtually all businesses require a comprehensive approach to productive maintenance.

- **Information systems:** We are moving from the information era to the era of decision-making and analysis, so it is not as important to have a lot of data, but know how to use the data and keep our communication systems, software, and hardware working in order to unite the elements of the system in a flow of information without interruption. Doing this, we achieve a competitive advantage.

Think back to the Strategy Weal in Chapter 2, where all elements, systems and tools will focus into one center – Purpose, Strategy, Vision, Mission and Values leading to the Lean Six Sigma Transformation.

4.2 A TRUE LEAN SIX SIGMA COMPANY

Designing a strong Lean Six Sigma Company always begins with the end in mind, the strategy design, organizational structure, and talent development system.

Designing a strong system, basically plans your transformation. Don't just copy another company; this will most likely not work out and fail. There may be internal voices that will say that Lean Six Sigma is not helpful. Therefore, a tailor-made approach for the four phases is the right method to use to design the *Lean Six Sigma Management* start or restart. Remember that problems and roadblocks will appear; just do the work and eliminate problems and roadblocks with the tools we have discussed previously. Remain focused and be patient, and good results will come.

What is a true Lean Six Sigma Company?

A Lean Six Sigma Company is a way of thinking and acting that makes it necessary for people to master the processes that produce correct results for employees, customers, and owners. It is a way of life that does not permit conformity and requires the best of each person to function properly and a high commitment by all of its members. It is a system that is built with great effort and that is maintained with the pride of being the best, taking into account that our work is what allows the development of our families and our nation.

A Lean Six Sigma Company provides a management system that focuses the efforts of teams at all levels to work primarily on what is necessary. Thus, it delivers value to the customer without stopping, by which it successfully integrates all areas of the company in a single focus of priorities.

The employees of a Lean Six Sigma Company will work and behave like the members of a symphony orchestra, playing a score in unison and harmony, creating high-level music.

The challenge for companies will be to teach everyone to play together as a team; for this, it requires creating a structure that achieves the necessary integration in a natural manner, with one score, which in this case is called a box score. Thus, the results mark the pace at which we should work and market priorities that dictate the rhythm of collaborative work.

Best practices can be implemented in all types of businesses, service organizations, and manufacturers of any size and maturity level.

"Lean Six Sigma Company is the way that companies should have always been designed, and now thanks to the knowledge and experience accumulated, everyone has it at their fingertips.

Services

Three out of four jobs that are performed are services. In this field, Lean Six Sigma is helping to not only provide better services, but also create life experiences for customers, significantly improving the cost, quality, and speed with which those services are performed. In fact, in manufacturing firms, much of the work done is considered internal services, such as maintenance, accounting, payroll, etc.

Examples of service companies that should implement Lean Company

Hotels, hospitals, restaurants, airports, government agencies, insurance companies, distributors, clinics, department stores, convenience stores, automotive shops, designers, carriers, universities, tourism, logistics, consulting, messaging, banks, marketing, professional services, etc.

Manufacturing

Manufacturing companies are totally changing the way they organize and train their personnel, plant design, and the way they produce, integrating in the value streams a whole team of people from different specialties and implementing the tools of continuous flow, production sequencing, mechanisms to detect errors, etc. This is to achieve more rapid delivery, with much better quality and lower costs, which result in increasing profits.

Examples of manufacturing companies that should implement *Lean Six Sigma Company*

Pharmaceutical , food, beverages, plastics, mining,construction, automotive, military, industrial, medical equipment, electronic, furniture, appliances, aerospace, foundry, decorative materials for textiles, packaging, construction materials, etc.

4.3 START OR RESTART THE LEAN SIX SIGMA COMPANY JOURNEY

A four phase is the best way to start or restart:

Phase 1. **Approach**
Phase 2. **Pilot**
Phase 3. **Value Stream Organization**
Phase 4. **Lean Six Sigma Company Organization**

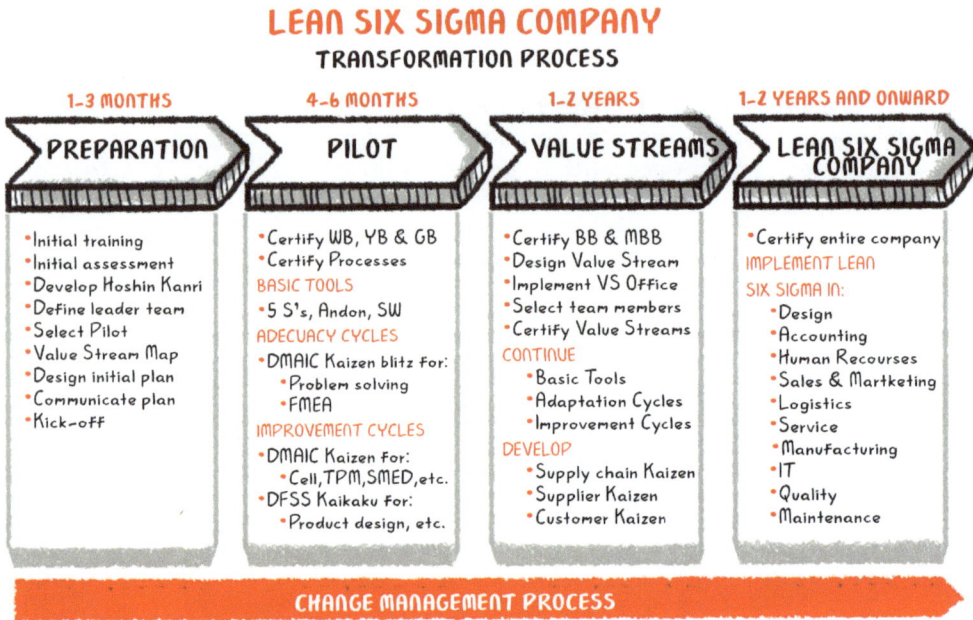

LEAN SIX SIGMA COMPANY
TRANSFORMATION PROCESS

1-3 MONTHS	4-6 MONTHS	1-2 YEARS	1-2 YEARS AND ONWARD
PREPARATION	**PILOT**	**VALUE STREAMS**	**LEAN SIX SIGMA COMPANY**
•Initial training	•Certify WB, YB & GB	•Certify BB & MBB	•Certify entire company
•Initial assessment	•Certify Processes	•Design Value Stream	IMPLEMENT LEAN
•Develop Hoshin Kanri	BASIC TOOLS	•Implement VS Office	SIX SIGMA IN:
•Define leader team	•5 S's, Andon, SW	•Select team members	•Design
•Select Pilot	ADECUACY CYCLES	•Certify Value Streams	•Accounting
•Value Stream Map	•DMAIC Kaizen blitz for:	CONTINUE	•Human Recourses
•Design initial plan	•Problem solving	•Basic Tools	•Sales & Martketing
•Communicate plan	•FMEA	•Adaptation Cycles	•Logistics
•Kick-off	IMPROVEMENT CYCLES	•Improvement Cycles	•Service
	•DMAIC Kaizen for:	DEVELOP	•Manufacturing
	•Cell, TPM, SMED, etc.	•Supply chain Kaizen	•IT
	•DFSS Kaikaku for:	•Supplier Kaizen	•Quality
	•Product design, etc.	•Customer Kaizen	•Maintenance

CHANGE MANAGEMENT PROCESS

Phase 1: Preparation
Duration: 1- 3 months

The Preparation Phase is to establish the pillars of the long-term philosophy of a Lean Six Sigma Company, prepare the necessary conditions for a successful transformation, and set the first actions for change management.

Preparation activities will develop a better understanding for all members of the company of why a Lean Six Sigma Company transformation is important and how it will bring benefits, even though resistance to change will be present.

Good preparation will help to get started and includes: management and project team training, reviewing company assessments, reviewing the company's Vision, Mission, Values, Strategic Planning, and Value Stream Mapping for definition of goals and expectations. This is time to involve the key employees and all stakeholders and think about how the future will be.

Main Activities
- Initial training for leaders so they will understand why becoming a Lean Six Sigma Company is an important strategy to consider for taking the company to the highest level
- Initial assessments to establish the starting status and define the gaps for improvements
- Develop a Hoshin Kanri to establish the vision, define strategies and projects, and define the key performance indicators
- Set up the team leader and define responsibilities
- Select pilot project based on priorities
- Set up a Master Plan
- Set up a Change Management Plan
- Prepare a Communication Plan
- Organize a Kick-off Ceremony to announce the *Lean Six Sigma Management Journey*

Participants
- CEO
- Managing Director(s)
- VP's
- Area Managers
- Human Resources Manager
- Project Team
- Support Team

Main Obstacles
- Resistance to change of some managers
- Fear of the unknown
- Postponement of plans and start

Main Advantages
- Challenge to change
- Need to learn something new
- New business dynamics and change

Phase 2: Pilot
Duration: 4 - 6 months

The Pilot Phase is simply a test or a trial of a new process, system, or transformation in a small and restricted area or business unit. It is the validation that the new system works as intended and provides the expected results. In this environment, we will make all the necessary changes, improvements and corrections until the expected results are achieved. The advantage of the pilot is that you work in a small and defined area and not throughout the whole system or company until the pilot phase shows consistent results.

During the Pilot Phase, the first victories will generate good feelings and motivation, demonstrating that Lean Six Sigma can help any type of process or industry.

Some basic tools could start being implemented in the rest of the company, such as 5 S's, Andon, Standardize Work, etc. Doing this could help to enhance the foundation and the motivation for the next phase, and most importantly, involve everyone!

This is one of the most important phases of the culture transformation, especially because we see if the company has the leaders and leadership necessary to manage the Lean Six Sigma Company of the future.

Main Activities
- Train and certificate White belts, Yellow belts and Green belts.
- Start 5 S's within the company
- Begin with Process Assessments (see also *LSSM - Fieldbook*)
- Perform Adequacy Cycles using Kaizen Blitz and FMEA's with some other tools to eliminate root causes of some recurrent problems
- Perform Improvement Cycles to help improve results through the application of Kaizen Events using DMAIC methodology and tools to design or re-design the pilot process and show outstanding results
- Review Opportunities for Industry 4.0/IIoT and test options
- Start the Value Stream office design and creation
- Use Box Score and floor meetings to start to analyze results continuously
- Implement Standard Work and other tools to sustain the culture
- Prepare the framework for the value stream phase
- Apply TPM, Continuous Flow, Poka Yoke, etc.
- Fully engage key members
- Start multi-task training for operators
- Start Lean Logistics between suppliers and customers

Participants
- Managing Director
- Area Managers
- Human Resources Managers
- Project and Support Teams
- Operators
- Process and quality engineers
- Maintenance personnel
- Supply Chain and Planning Department

Main Obstacles
- Resistance to change of personnel in general
- Incorrect application of knowledge
- Lack of dedication of the time required

Main Advantages
- Company begins to see some positive results
- Initiate internal competitiveness for better results
- Improves teamwork
- Better understanding of the techniques and structure
- High Interest for more positive results in other areas
- Management is totally committed
- Establishes the base for Lean Six Sigma Certification

Phase 3 - Value Stream Organization
Duration: 1 – 2 years

In the Value Stream Phase, the organizational structure becomes the foundation of the implementation because it establishes a way of working managed by processes, not in functional departments. We will now apply what we learned from the previous pilot phase to the entire value stream.

Lean Six Sigma for accounting, logistics, procurement, and all support processes related to the value streams are included in the implementation to create the systemic approach and increase the benefits of the transformation.

During this phase, the company will experience a great team transformation that requires forming, storming, adaptation, and performance steps for advancement. Most of the time this will be hard, but after the first six months, we have seen great results and total integration nearly all the time. This is when teams will be including and excluding members based on natural selection as self-guided teams.

Main Activities
- Certification training continues to the next level of knowledge
- Integration of Industry 4.0/IIoT elements in the value stream
- Analysis of the results achieved
- Full application of Lean Six Sigma strategic tools
- Full pull production/service system is developed
- Special Kaizen events held with customers and suppliers
- Projects started with great variability in applying statistics
- Lean accounting now includes:
    » Management accounting
    » Financial Accounting
    » Operational accounting
- Introduction of value stream manager
- Organizational design by value streams is designed and implemented
- Personnel assigned to value streams
- Use of lean and sigma tactical tools
- DMAIC in all improvement and problem solving projects
- Introduction of the lean office

- Cost accounting integrated into the value streams
- Lean Budget is implemented
- Financial planning integrated with sales and value streams
- Multi-skills certification (Cross training)
- New incentive methods are integrated
- Integrated logistics with suppliers and customers
- Everyone contributes with improvement ideas
- Strategic tools are practiced by leaders of all levels

Participants
- Managing Director
- Area Managers
- Human Resources Managers
- Project and Support Teams
- Operators
- Process and quality engineers
- Maintenance personnel
- Accounting and IT
- Supply Chain, Planning and Logistics
- Marketing and Sales
- R&D

Main Obstacles
- Lack of integration between value stream team
- Information flow not connected to all team members
- Possible use of previous methods of control
- Resistance to change due to loss of authority
- Possible detection of lack of capacity for leadership
- Conflicts of interests between departments
- Limitations of authority to make decisions

Main Advantages
- Results show a clear reduction in costs and increase in ROI
- Better communication and understanding between people
- Teamwork allows improvement of interpersonal relationships
- There is better understanding of the way forward
- The information is much clearer and easier to use
- All employees start understanding the benefits of the Lean Six Sigma philosophy
- Begin Value Stream Assessments (see *LSSM - Fieldbook*)

One of our most important clients decided to implement Lean Six Sigma company wide as their most important strategy. After two years of hard work and excellent top management commitment, they are now able to develop great results from multi-tasking teams organized by Value Streams where collaboration among various departments are paying off by doubling their capacity, reducing their cost significantly every year, and offering excellent products to their clients.

Phase 4 - Lean Six Sigma Company Organization
Duration: 1 - 2 years and onward

A Lean Six Sigma Company is characterized by having achieved the commitment for learning and teaching as one of its greatest values and has established a knowledge management system that allows the organization to have documented control of problems, improvements, means of prevention, and everything that is relevant to the correct operation of the organization. Also, the working conditions at all levels of the company demonstrate the firm commitment to provide value to society.

During this phase, the *Lean Six Sigma Company* assessment for certification opens the opportunity for every process of the company to become agile and productive. The company develops a plan with specific activities to be performed in order to achieve a systemic approach by integrating all the elements or departments into a single improvement culture. Everyone is learning from each other and participating in all processes to help to improve them, providing the opportunity to learn how a real *Lean Six Sigma Company* should operate.

Main Activities
- Apply strategic tools company-wide
- Identify opportunities in other processes: logistics, accounting, sales, design
- Develop improvement projects in every process around the main constrain of the company
- Continuous breakdown paradigms
- Application of Industry 4.0/IIoT applications to all areas of the company where there is an advantage to do it
- Extensive use of Lean Six Sigma strategic and tactical tools within company
- Publish operational and financial results
- The company has its own university where the critical knowledge is taught
- The company works to become the industry benchmark

- Lean Six Sigma projects are the foundation of maturity
- Lean Six Sigma certification: company-wide, value streams and processes
- Teams become self-guided
- Top management team focuses 80% on outside the company
- Ongoing processes of the entire company are certified continuously

Participants
- CEO and Management team
- Managing Directors and VP's
- Area Managers
- Guidance Team
- Value stream managers and support teams
- Value stream members
- Project Team
- Support Team

Main Obstacles
- Turnover of top management
- New managers without the vision or preparation
- Uncertainty in the global business environment
- Reliance on past successes (you need to stay persistent and sustain results)
- Not renewing or aligning strategy, products, and operating model when necessary (Business Model CANVAS and Hoshin Kanri)

Main Advantages
- A renewed work culture that is always ready for change
- Shared leadership
- Tools and knowledge
- Clear and constant understanding of goals and objectives
- *Lean Six Sigma Management* is a successful way of thinking
- Lean Six Sigma Certification gives clients and employees the confidence of working with the best in class by maximizing people and company potential

A retail company was implementing a Lean Six Sigma Transformation and faced a lot of resistance in the Preparation Phase. This is not uncommon and requires that top management stay close to the teams. Rather than the one to three months planned, it took the company over one year to get prepared and begin the Pilot Phase. It is important to realize that you may need to take two steps back to make sure the employees understand the change and benefits and follow your plans. Neglecting the situation can make the transformation fail.

Characteristics of a true Lean Six Sigma Company

- Customer focused
- Usually very low cost
- Highest productivity and Overall Equipment Effectivness (OEE)
- Lowest scrap rate
- Lowest inventory
- Lean Six Sigma in all processes
- Lowest customer complaint rate
- Best trained employees
- Continuous Improvement culture
- Track results per shift, day, week, month, quarter, and year
- Disciplined
- Goal focused
- Processes, value streams, and company are certified

4.4 LEAN SIX SIGMA COMPANY CERTIFICATION AND BENCHMARKS

Companies have worked hard to implement different degrees of Lean Six Sigma in their organization. Unfortunately, management typically doesn't know where the level of Lean Six Sigma is compared to other companies in their Lean Six Sigma Journey. In order to measure and compare the Level or Maturity, there are two options:

I. Assessment done by Lean Six Sigma Organizations
II. 3rd. Body Lean Six Sigma Certification

I. Assessments done by Lean Six Sigma Organizations
One option is internal assessments that we spoke about in Chapter 2 using different assessment formats. This is actually a great way to measure and compare with other departments, sites, or plants of the organization. The only downside is that you can't compare with other organizations.

The internal assessments are usually:
- Certification of People
- Support Processes
- Value Streams
- Lean Company (the whole organization)
- Industry 4.0 / IIoT Industrial Internet of Things (level of integration in all previous assessments)

In the path to become a *Lean Six Sigma Company*, we need to prepare and ensure that the right knowledge and processes are in place. These will be certified step by step through four categories of certification:

- **Certification of People:** when individuals are trained and demonstrate knowledge in White Belt, Yellow Belt, Green Belt, Black Belt and Master Black Belt, they receive a certificate

- **Certification of a Support Process:** when each process meets the requirements, it can be certified and recertified annually with random checks conducted by Master Black Belts experts to ensure that the methods are sustained and that the tools function properly on a regular basis by the personnel that operate them

- **Certification of a Value Streams:** when all the processes of the value stream have achieved a certain level of progress collectively and have demonstrated results and habitual use of them, they can be certified. Certification of value chains is reviewed every two years to check the sustainment and progress

- **Certification of a whole Company - Corporation:** when the strategy, vision, mission, values, the value streams of a business and all supportive processes and people of a company have been certified, it is certified as a Lean Company

In every certification level mentioned before, we will measure the maturity level of Industry 4.0 / IIoT Industrial Internet of Things.

Certifying your company will help you to understand at which level of maturity the company is currently and define an action plan to succeed in the culture transformation.

"New" Third-Party Lean Six Sigma Company Certifications

A recognized, independent, full-service provider for certifications in Lean Six Sigma will evaluate the Lean Six Sigma Company processes, systems and services, their sound implementation, and their efficacy by looking at their KPI's compared to previous months and years. The key is the neutrality and high quality of these certified companies.

The certification usually takes 3-5 days depending on the size of the company, verification after one year usually takes 2-3 days, depending on the size of the company. The score achieved will determine your efficacy level as a Lean Six Sigma Company. The minimum score is 700 points out of maximum 1000 points.

The goal of this certification is not to just look at your processes, systems, and services to see if they are implemented or not compared to your procedures, but is whether or not these tools and procedures are providing you with improved KPI's compared to the previous year.

The difference between a certification and a verification.

- **Certification** enables you to demonstrate that your processes, systems, or services are compliant with the international Lean Six Sigma standards. After a successful certification you will receive a certification plate depending on the level (steel, bronze, silver or gold)

- **Verification** enables you to verify that your processes, systems, or services are compliant with the international Lean Six Sigma standards

A strong certification company will provide the following benefits:

- Receiving an official certification document
- Compares/benchmarks results between global companies
- Rate you so that you have the opportunity to improve year by year
- Let you know your strengths and weaknesses
- Makes sure you work on the deviations with agreed-upon deadlines in order to be certified quickly
- Will do pre-assessments and prepare you for the certification

When a food company started implementing Lean Six Sigma companywide, it was difficult for them to understand how far from world-class they were and evaluate their real progress from the many projects and efforts around their Lean Six Sigma transformation. However, when they started the Lean Six Sigma company assessment for certification, the whole company was evaluated. Every team from Value Stream and Support Process had their own action plan and developed people and actions to have a guideline for fully transforming their company to produce an outstanding result as a system and promote an agile culture.

Please look into the LSSM – Fieldbook for more examples, formats, and Information

4.5 KEY POINTS

1. Use the 4 Phase approach to get (re)start Lean Six Sigma
2. Don't be surprised by roadblocks and problems, as a leader just stay focused and supportive to solve the problems and roadblocks with your teams
3. A Lean Six Sigma Company is the way that companies should have always been designed, and now thanks to the knowledge and experience accumulated, everyone has it at their fingertips
4. There are huge opportunities available to implement Lean Six Sigma in different industries, as well as in ours
5. A Certification of a Lean Six Sigma Company by a professional third-party company is an added value to verify where we are and what is missing compared to the best in the industry
6. Lean Six Sigma Company is a never ending continuous improvement

Please add your additional Key Points:

_____
_____
_____
_____
_____
_____
_____
_____
_____
_____
_____
_____

CHAPTER 5

5. STRONG BENEFITS AND RESULTS OF A LEAN SIX SIGMA TRANSFORMATION

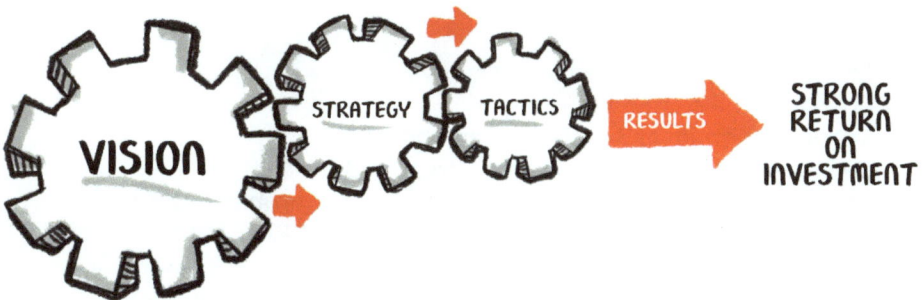

5.1 INTRODUCTION

Any industry has problems to solve, processes to improve, and people to develop in order to succeed in the long term. We need to improve day by day not just in manufacturing or service processes, but in every process of the company, including customer service, sales, marketing, accounting, logistics, IT, and Maintenance. If every department or process is aligned with the company's strategy and vision, the overall result will be very efficient and productive with more engaged and committed people as part of the transformation process.

LEAN SIX SIGMA APPLIES TO ANY PROCESS — Customer Service, Manufacturing, Accounting, Operations, Sales, HR & IT

... AND TO ANY INDUSTRY — Healthcare, Hi-Tech, Government, Retail, Finance, Hospitality

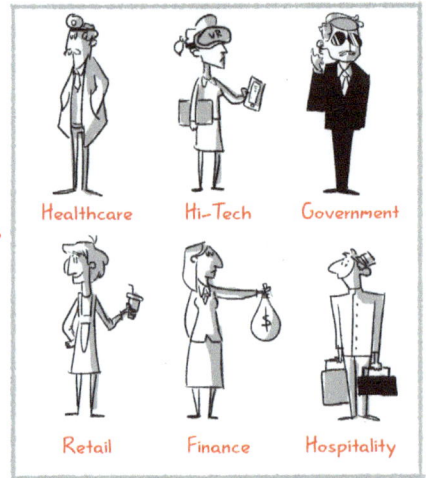

Every industry should improve systematically as a whole. The transformation will provide incredible results and benefits:

- Change in customer satisfaction and experience
- Change in the company results
- Change in employee satisfaction and behavior
- Change in the way the company is organized
- Change in the way people generate ideas, solve problems, and make decisions
- Change in the commitment of every single person in the company
- Change in how we deal with suppliers and include them in the process
- Change in the way we are perceived by all stakeholders, including the market

From all these changes, benefits will come in different ways. Looking back over the last three decades, where we supported over 500 companies in more than 20 different industries, we have always seen companies improving processes and results, resulting in big benefits from a Lean Six Sigma Transformation.

5.2 HARD AND SOFT BENEFITS FROM A LEAN SIX SIGMA TRANSFORMATION

Hard Benefits

Let's look at the hard benefits as measurable results achieved through the implementation of the Lean Six Sigma Transformation. Remember that the Lean Six Sigma Transformation is a long-term journey that is going to produce results in the short, medium, and long term. However, if the short-term benefits don't come as fast as you expected, please don't quit. Be patient; it's just a matter of time and they will certainly come.

Here a summary of hard benefits:
- Increase in throughput
- Cost reduction in all areas, such as sales/marketing, overhead, manufacturing, quality, maintenance, logistics etc.
- Increase in profit
- Reduction in use of space
- Inventory reduction
- Cash flow improvement
- Capacity increase
- Quality improvement
- Cost avoidance
- Capital expenditure avoidance
- Process efficiency

While every business and every industry is different, when leaders decide to work in a Lean Six Sigma culture, everything starts changing in a very positive way. Hard benefits are important and key for managers and investors to keep interest and be willing to invest further in this long-term philosophy. Keep close track of your daily and monthly KPI's and you will start seeing improving results and benefits. Also, the employees will be looking closely at the Score boards.

If they see Indicators are improving due to the actions implemented, they will start supporting it.

Nevertheless, if revenues haven't increased and cost and inventories haven't decreased after a few months or a year at the longest, then the program needs to be reviewed immediately. In all the years we have supported companies in making a Lean Six Sigma transformation, the results have always been drastic and sustainable improvements if it has been implemented with a clear plan that includes all employees using the tools correctly and working day by day to improve processes.

Soft benefits

Soft benefits are defined as non-monetary benefits, but they are just as important as hard benefits. Actually, for the long-term business, they are even more important in order to assure and sustain the achievements of the hard benefits.

There are always soft benefits achieved in any implementation and in every project. They are also very important because they influence employee behavior and whether or not they think that the company is a good place to work.

Nobody likes to work in a place where there are is no challenge, committed leadership, or safe working conditions.

Some of the most important Soft Benefits are:

- Increased customer satisfaction
- Improvement in internal and external communication
- Increased employee satisfaction
- Reduction in employee turnover
- Safety improvements
- Increase in improvement ideas from individuals and teams
- Increase in improvement Ideas executed
- Continuous improvement culture implemented
- Improved discipline
- Employees following processes
- Sticking to company values and commitments

Lean Six Sigma philosophy increases employee morale due to the following three key elements that every team develops by working on the transformation:

- **Achievement** – everybody feels great when the job is done well and the expected goals have been achieved.

- **Belonging** – this is a human need that is experienced when the Value Stream Structure is implemented and the company is not managed by departments anymore, which reduces the level of stress and allows better results due to strong team integration.

- **Contribution** – every individual is motivated when they participate in adaptation and improvement cycles by giving ideas and working to implement them, but also when leaders recognize the higher results achieved by teams compared to individual achievements.

Remember that communication improvement is one of the biggest benefits of a Lean Six Sigma culture. Every strategic and tactical tool has a component related with communication improvement, so please keep that in mind as part of your job as a leader.

5.3 ROI – RETURN ON INVESTMENT FOR A LEAN SIX SIGMA TRANSFORMATION

The Return on Investment (ROI) is a crucial KPI for any large transformation. If we invest hundreds of thousands of Euros or U.S. dollars in a continuous improvement program, we want to see good returns coming back. Needless to say, many companies have invested large sums of money without having seen any return on their investment and thus abandoned the program. On the other hand, we know many companies that not only had an important ROI but continue to remain leaders in their respective industries.

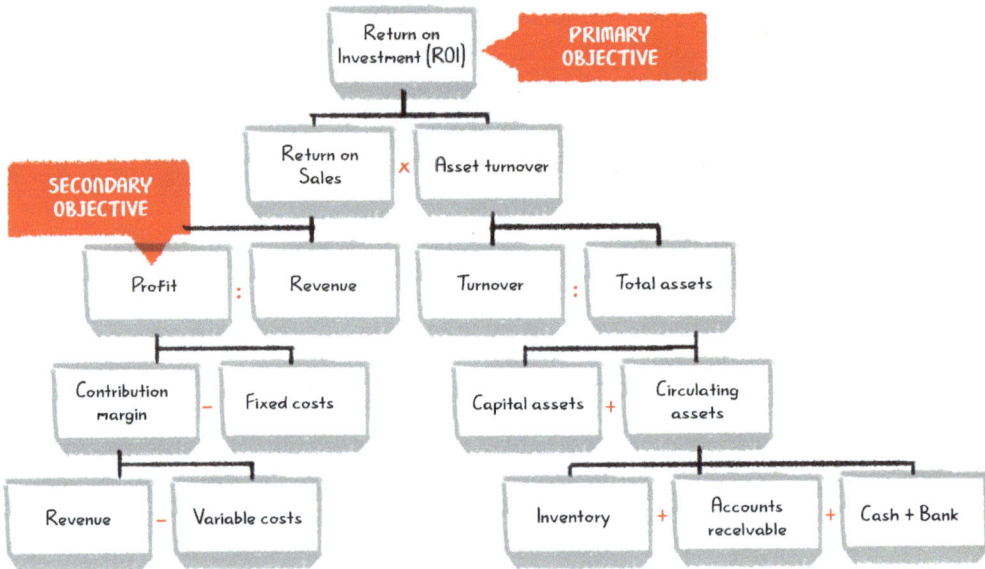

Originally developed by DuPont, the ROI model is now in worldwide use. It's a fast, convenient financial measure that helps leaders understand the relationship between profit and sales.

$$\frac{\text{Net Income (of profit)}}{\text{Sales}} \times \frac{\text{Sales}}{\text{Total assets}} = \frac{\text{Net Income}}{\text{Total assets}} = \text{ROI}$$

We have seen our customers' ROI going from 2:1 within two years to greater than 10:1 in best case scenarios, which means that for every Euro or USD they invested in a Lean Six Sigma Program, they would get 10 back!

The difference between the low ROI companies compared to the higher ones may occur for the following reasons:

Low to no ROI return:

- Not really believing in the Lean Six Sigma philosophy
- No alignment with Vision, Mission, Values, and Strategy
- Unclear goals
- Continuously changing priorities
- Only selecting one Lean Six Sigma project with little to no improvements, so some effort was expended for a small return
- No consequences if the company implements or does not implement Lean Six Sigma
- Insufficiently trained and certified employees in Yellow Belt, Green Belt, Black Belt and Master Black Belt
- Management is not leading or even behind the transformation
- Key Lean executives or professionals left the company

Companies that are thriving in Lean Six Sigma transformation have improved over 3-5 years after starting the journey and are experiencing an EBITA in the low range of between 10-15% from sales turnover up to a greater than 50% from sales turnover. Again, the key is that *Lean Six Sigma Management* is part of a company-wide transformation.

What high ROI companies do:

- Lean Six sigma transformation is an integral part of the Vision, Mission, Values, and Strategy.
- Management is 100% behind and trained in Lean Six Sigma Philosophy.
- Enough people are trained in order to have resources for the projects.
- Assessments are done and a strong system is designed.
- Preparation, Pilot with a Value Stream and Lean Organization
- People hired with a Lean Attitude
- Lean Six Sigma Projects very visible, reviewed every week

We can only recommend implementing Lean Six Sigma in any company and industry because there is really no downside.

5.4 TRANSFORMATION CASES, BENEFITS AND RESULTS

In this section, we are going to review some real transformation cases from different industries and company sizes that used Lean Six Sigma as a transformation to improve their situation. Each case was very different and unique, but the methodology of the transformation process was the same.

Company owners, managers, and leaders usually looked back and said, *"Why didn't we do it sooner?* Now that we achieved these results, *what else can we do to improve even more?"*

**"What if we don't change at all...
and something magical just happens?"**

We will take a close look into five cases of Lean Six Sigma Transformation:

1. Bank – Loan process
2. Turbine Manufacturing – for paint spraying industry
3. Healthcare - Clinic
4. Automobile – Car Dealer Service Center
5. Packaging – for Pharma and Medtech Industry

CASE 1: BANK – Loan Processing

This is a case of a small bank that urgently needed to improve their loan processing. They needed to increase capacity, improve quality, and drastically reduce cost.

KEY FACTS

BEFORE
- Capacity = 120 loans processed per month
- Low revenue generated
- High fixed cost per loan processed
- Constant rework due to errors
- Waiting time in the whole value stream
- Deficient communication among departments

AFTER 6 MONTHS
- Capacity = 312 loans processed per month
- Strong revenue growth
- Cost per loan decrease more than 40%
- Same number of staff
- Almost three times faster process
- Increased profits by 22% per loan
- Strongly improved communication

Analyzing any financial process is very interesting due to all the types of interactions from different departments and people.

Initial situation
As every step of the process is performed by different people and departments, there are many delays, and the bottleneck seems to vary continually.

- High variability in the total time to process each loan
- Not enough people trained in the different tasks great deal of paper work for each loan
- Constant reworks due to mistakes
- Computer systems are not designed to allow working as a team
- The challenge in loan processing is that all loans are treated the same way regardless of the risk, so some loans that require more time to process delay other less risky loans
- Collecting data and documentation is not standardized

Transformation
After developing the Value Stream Map and identifying the main sources of waste, the following actions were taken:

- Housekeeping in office areas and in documentation
- Cross-training matrix and certification program to develop multi-skilled people
- Software development to upload the documents directly by the client
- Implement continuous flow by creating loan teams by level of risk
- Assign a leader to be the only contact with the client to do the follow up

CASE 2: MANUFACTURING – Turbine Manufacturing

This is a case of a turbine manufacturing company that produces turbines for the painting industry. Their situation was so critical that the company would go out of business if drastic actions were not taken.
They needed to increase throughput, improve quality, and drastically reduce costs and delivery time.

KEY FACTS

BEFORE
- Capacity = 20 – 30 machines per day
- Backlog = 80,000 USD
- Inventory = More than 2 Million USD
- Delivery time = 3 – 4 weeks
- High cost per unit
- Constant rework

AFTER 1 YEAR
- Capacity = 50 – 70 machines per day
- Backlog = 0 USD
- Inventory = 650,000 USD
- Delivery time = 2 days maximum
- Cost per unit reduction = < 23%
- Quality increase > 95%

Initial Situation

As a result, of the economic recession of 2009, many companies closed during 2010, and other companies had to find new ways to continue in business. Customers were not willing to wait more than two weeks to receive a turbine and continue to pay for their supplier's inefficiencies. The following findings were discovered at the beginning of the project.

- High employee turnover
- High inventory level in finished goods and work in process
- Low cash flow
- Long delivery times: from 3 to 4 weeks after the order was received
- High defect rate and rework
- Long distances for material transportation and people doing work in plant
- Specialized workers doing only one or two functions

Transformation

The owner of the company took the initiative and decided to train everybody in Lean Six Sigma. After a thorough housekeeping workshop, the entire company applied 5 S's, including offices, manufacturing work area, and the warehouse. Some of the activities during the one-year transformation were:

- Hoshin Kanri and Box Score, Gemba walks
- 5 S's implementation in the entire company
- Andon boards on the shop floor
- Talent development system with cross-training matrix and compensation model
- Complete reorganization of the company layout into cellular manufacturing instead of departments
- Pull system managed by Kanban was designed and implemented

CASE 3: HEALTHCARE – Clinic

This is a case of a small health clinic in the Houston area, whose leadership team was desperate and needed to act quickly in order to improve the capacity and service to customers.

KEY FACTS

BEFORE	AFTER 18 MONTHS
• Capacity = 10,000 patients per month	• Capacity = 15,000 patients per month
• Waiting time = 2 hours in average	• Waiting time = 15 min in average
• Net Promoter Score (NPS) = 20%	• Net Promoter Score (NPS) = 56%
• Constant complaints	• Strongly reduced complaint rate

Initial Situation

Improving was not just a choice for this small clinic in Houston, they needed to increase their capacity by 50% due to a demand from a major hospital that was their partner in the area. Also, their customer service was poor, and customers were complaining about waiting up to two hours, even though certain services were good.

After conducting the Lean Six Sigma initial assessment, we detected the following improvement opportunities:

- Net Promoter Score (NPS) = 20% which means that out of 100 patients, only 20 would come back or recommend the service to relatives or friends
- Lack of integration and communication among departments
- Patients without appointments were mixed with patients with appointments, generating confusion and long waiting times
- Long check-in process due to time needed to find medical charts
- Client's complaints

Transformation
- All employees received Lean Six Sigma Healthcare training
- Strategic tools implemented:
  » Hoshin Kanri
  » Box Score meetings
  » Lean Accounting implemented
  » Gemba Walks daily

- Kaizen Events for improvement using tactical tools:
  - » Check-in process implementing 5 S's, Visual control, and quick setup for incoming patients
  - » Continuous flow for patients with appointments
  - » Dedicated flow for patients without appointments
  - » Pharmacy 5 S's, re-layout, and Kanban system to replenish medications
  - » Accounts receivable 5 S's, Project Management, SMED, Poka Yoke, and Visual Control (Andon)
  - » Lean Cost Accounting to understand the real cost per patient

CASE 4: AUTOMOBILE – Car Dealer Service Center

This is a case of an automobile dealer's car service center whose customers were very unhappy with the service provided, so that they were losing customers to the competition. They needed to improve the speed of service, increase capacity, increase throughput, improve quality, decrease customer complaints, and drastically reduce cost and processing time.

KEY FACTS

BEFORE
- Delivery time = 2 – 3 days delivery time
- Not enough capacity
- Customer complaints
- Constant reworks

AFTER 1.5 YEARS
- Delivery time = 2 hours
- 45% increase in capacity with the same resources
- 28% reduction in cost per service
- Became the Number 1 car dealer service center in 6 months

Initial Situation

The customers were very unsatisfied due to the long maintenance service process, generating delivery times of two to three days in the best case for simple, regular car maintenance, generating a poor customer experience and rating.

Initial situation had the following problems:

- Inefficient service appointment system
- Poor scheduling process with constant changes and contradictions
- Lack of spare parts for the scheduled car maintenance
- Poor customer service communication to update every customer when something was late
- Internal bottleneck in the regular car maintenance due to lack of parts
- Spare parts warehouse totally unorganized

Transformation
- Service department personnel trained in Lean service
- KPI definition for service department and for service scheduling
- Developed Andon board for the shop floor to communicate and assign the work

- Kaizen to implement Lean warehouse and spare parts team delivery to workstations
- 5 min. meeting on the shop floor with mechanics and spare parts team
- Kaizen for quick preparation of materials and spare parts for scheduled maintenance
- Kaizen for Continuous Flow from check-in, receiving, online paperwork process, maintenance job, car wash, and customer service
- Implementation of Gemba Walks and Leader Standard Work

Other results
- In this case, it was very interesting to see how the morale improved when the team saw the first results and received good reviews from clients.
- Customer Net Promoter Score increased from 25% to 60% in six months
- More than 30% increase in profits

Case 5. MANUFACTURING - Pharma Packaging

This is a case of a pharma packaging manufacturer who was struggling in recent years to keep pace with the changing market demands. This is a highly regulated market whose customers wanted the best and consistent quality at competitive prices.

KEY FACTS

BEFORE
- Sales decrease for years
- Lost loyal costumers
- High inventory level
- OEE = 62%
- Low single digit EBIT
- Investment rate low

AFTER 2.5 YEARS
- Sales increase 35%
- 95% of customers recovered
- Inventory reduction 40% RM, WIP 85%, FG 35%
- OEE = 87%
- EBIT increased by high double digits
- First Pass rate 92%

Situation

The company had been developing primary packaging containers for the pharma industry for years and was the market leader in the region. However, in the recent years, the company became complacent, arrogant to customers, lead-times became unpredictable for customers, quality diminished, earnings were lower with a downward trend, a stronger competitor appeared key, people and customers started to abandon the company. Investment lowered, due to lack of return and insecure future. Many different action plans were put in place, including strict cost cutting plans, but unfortunately, the results did not improve and even worsened due to incorrect cost cutting and short-term thinking.

Transformation

The management team asked for external help to support the recovery. After a thorough assessment in all key areas, they decided to turn things around by implementing a Lean Six Sigma transformation.

Master Plan Key Topics and Tools used:
- Company assessment
- Communication – Change Management Process to all employees about the past, present, and future
- Training in Lean and Six Sigma
- Start with 5 S's

- Hoshin Kanri – Box Score
- TPM on all key equipment
- Kaizen Events
- Rigorous waste reduction
- A3 and Ishikawa
- Standard Operating Procedures
- Visual Management – Andon
- Kanban
- Gemba Walks
- Six Sigma
- Continuous employee and customer surveys
- New supply chain concept
- Changed to the most rigorous certification company

The company had a very hard first year of recovery in order to align and synchronize all priorities.

Other results:
Fortunately, the company turned things around very well and again became the market leader. Some key achievements after 2.5 years were:
- Quality complaints reduced by 93% from 30 per month to 1-2 per month
- 5 S's implemented in all areas
- Visual Management with boards in all key areas
- Regular Gemba Walks and all meetings on the floor
- Sales increased by 35%, when the market was growing only 3%/year
- TPM on 50% of the lines systematic training in all areas
- Innovation and large Investment in new technologies
- EBIT increased to high double digits

We still hear back regularly today from the company that they achieved some new best-in-class results. Additional tools have been implemented and processes are running smoothly. It is all about people and stable processes, implementing a rigorous and systematic continuous improvement system and culture, while working on the processes every day.

5.5 WRAP-UP AND CLOSING

As we come to the end of this book, you have seen that we have not reinvented Lean Six Sigma; this was already done years ago. Instead, we have learned how to use it over the years, how to implement it successfully, sometimes fine-tune some concepts and utilize the tools with leaders and teams to achieve the company's vision and goals.

We are very proud of the fact that we have been able to help many companies and organizations implement the true Lean Six Sigma Company concepts. Through leadership, these companies have achieved outstanding results, some of them even achieving best-in-class level in their industry.

We learned that when the tools and concepts are working together, it is like musicians playing together in a symphony orchestra. Sometimes the sequence of certain tools needs some variation, some fine-tuning. Sometimes a company specific plan is required, but the goal remains the same, and at the end, we achieved the desired results.

When you and your team start a Lean Six Sigma Journey, all methodologies, tools, and every process will be subject to be careful study to identify bottlenecks and any other type of waste to be able to figure out how to set up the transformation.

One of the major objectives of Lean Six Sigma is to move from achieving maximum capacity to achieving optimal productivity and therefore be more profitable.

Leaders need to develop learning organizations, open for new discoveries either from outside or from inside the company. It's really all about a clear vision with the end in mind, a solid plan, a full commitment from the top management down through the whole organization. Obstacles and roadblocks will appear as in every project. The key as a leader is to remove the roadblocks, help the teams review priorities, and stay focused

We are committed to help you to a restart or start a *Lean Six Sigma Management* journey.

There is really NO downside, except by not doing it, you miss out on all the benefits we mentioned in the previous chapters.

On the other hand, if we execute it poorly or not well planned, then it will fail! We could even say that to not starting the Lean Six Sigma Journey will put your business at risk in the future. The digital age and new technologies like Industry 4.0/IIoT will require strong and lean processes. So, just get started with the journey.

We are very proud that we have had tremendous opportunities to support, lead, and improve so many companies and plants globally and have been able to achieve great results in customer satisfaction, quality improvement, employee satisfaction, and huge amounts of savings that helped invest in better technologies, processes, and training. This obviously could not have been achieved without strong and committed leaders and their teams.

Thanks again to all the leaders, professionals, and teams for allowing us to help and transform their companies.

If you have questions or uncertainty, feel free to contact us true *Linked In.*

In order to support your journey, don't forget to also get the complementary ***Lean Six Sigma - Management Fieldbook,*** which will have additional formats, examples, and information on how to implement tools and improvements. Don't miss it!

We hope you enjoyed reading this book. Please let us know how your Lean Six Sigma Journey is doing and results are progressing.

*A True Lean Company is a lifelong marathon and not a sprint –
Enjoy the journey! Luis and Carlo*

BIBLIOGRAPHY

The Machine That Changed the World: The Story of Lean Production- Toyota's Secret Weapon in the Global Car Wars That Is Now Revolutionizing World Industry Paperback – March 13, 2007by James P. Womack, Daniel T. Jones, Daniel Roos

Toyota Kata: Managing People for Improvement, Adaptiveness and Superior Results Aug 4, 2009 by Mike Rother Leading Change, With a New Preface by the Author . Nov 6, 2012 by John P. Kotter

The Toyota Way: 14 Management Principles from the World's Greatest – January 7, 2004 by Jeffrey K. Liker

The Goal: A Process of Ongoing Improvement – June 1, 2014 by Eliyahu M. Goldratt & Jeff Cox

The Startup Way: How Modern Companies Use Entrepreneurial Management to Transform Culture and Drive Long-Term Growth. Oct 17, 2017 by Eric Ries

Business Model Generation: A Handbook for Visionaries, Game Changers, and Challengers. Jul 13, 2010 by Alexander Osterwalder and Yves Pigneur

Scrum for Dummies: Apr 20, 2015by Mark C. Layton

Scrum: The Art of Doing Twice the Work in Half the Time. Sep 30, 2014 by Jeff Sutherland and JJ Sutherland

Gemba Walks Expanded: 2nd Edition. Oct 22, 2013 by Jim Womack and John Shook

Industry 4.0: The Industrial Internet of Things. Jun 28, 2016 by Alasdair Gilchrist

Lean Company: Más allá de la manufactura 2015 by Luis Socconini

Lean Manufacturing Paso a Paso: 2007 by Luis Socconini

Developing Leadership Skills 27: What is Leaders Standard Work? - Module 3 Section 9. Apr 5, 2017 by Jeffrey Liker and George Trachilis

The Talent Management Handbook: Second Edition. Creating a Sustainable Competitive Advantage by Selecting, Developing, and Promoting the Best People. Dec 1, 2010 by Lance A. Berger and Dorothy R. Berger

Hoshin Kanri: Policy Deployment for Successful TQM 1st Edition by Yoji Akao

Kaizen: The Key To Japan's Competitive Success. Nov 1, 1986 by Masaaki Imai

Introduction to TPM: Total Productive Maintenance (Preventative Maintenance Series) (English and Japanese Edition). Oct 1, 1988 by Seiichi Nakajima and Norman Bodek

"Felix Oberholzer, HBS, Strategy: Building + Sustaining Competitive Advantage 2017"

Quick Changeover for Operators: The SMED System (The Shopfloor Series) (Volume 3) Jun 3, 1996 by Shigeo Shingo

Kanban: Step-By-Step Agile Guide Designed To Help Teams Working Together More Effectively Sep 20, 2017 by Harry Altman

Seis-Sigma / Six Sigma: Metadologia y tecnicas / Methodology and Techniques (Spanish Edition) Jun 30, 2005 by Edgardo J. Escalante

Managing to Learn: Using the A3 Management Process to Solve Problems, Gain Agreement, Mentor and Lead. Jun 1, 2008 by John Shook and Jim Womack

Implement Industry 4.0: Leading Change in Manufacturing and Operation, 2017 by Mahnen John, MIT.

ISBN: 978-069-2951-64-4

9 780692 951644